TEACHING SMARTER

www.teachingsmarter.net

Dozens of **Practical & Easy** ideas
you can use in your classroom
...starting tomorrow!

Teaching Smarter

Sandy LaBelle

ESTARR PUBLISHING

Second edition 2001
Third edition 2004

ISBN 0-9676831-0-6

Printed by Gorham Printing, Rochester, Washington USA

Cover photograph by Kevin Patterson. Models: Jeanette, Jason, Tyler, Gene, and (the twins) Sherise and Denise

Dedication

This book is dedicated to my husband, Dennis.
Without his help and encouragement,
I would have never seriously started this journey.
He was the one who told me,

" Sometimes P.O.E. (Plenty of Experience)
is at least as valuable as a Ph.D."

Acknowledgments

I would like to take a moment to recognize just a few of the many people who have helped me "push my comfort zone,"

My husband, DENNIS, was the first to encourage me and supports me still on a daily basis.

ROBERTA PUGSLEY, the Career Center Director at Tahoma High School, was the person who helped me become a presenter at my first state conference.

SANDY SCHWARTZ, Vocational Director for the Kent School District, was the first person outside of my own district to believe in *Teaching Smarter* and hire me as a consultant.

SHERRYL GUNNELS-PERRY, the Managing Partner for Future Choice, was one of my first business world mentors and became a new friend. We have had numerous conversations which have helped me grow. Sherryl helped edit this book.

ELIZABETH MATHEWSON, Secondary Level Curriculum Support person for the Tahoma School District (now retired), is the right brain to my left brain. Prior to her curriculum job, she taught English for many years. She hired me to teach new teachers the techniques of *Teaching Smarter*, then provided me with feedback on how successfully the techniques were working for our new folks. She encouraged me frequently. She edited my book.

Thank you so much to these people and to the many others who have been so supportive! I could go on for several more pages, but I know you are anxious to begin the journey of reading this book. So, I conclude with a "Thank you so very much!" to the others who have helped me and encouraged me to continue sharing.

Contents

PART ONE

Contents, cont'd

Contents, cont'd

part one

Before we can expect teachers
to embrace systemic change,
we need to offer *specific* techniques
to help reduce their stress and fatigue.

CHAPTER 1

How did *Teaching Smarter* come about?

I want to thank you for beginning this journey. This book is written in a conversational tone, so get a cup of coffee, relax and let's begin to explore how together we can help you become a more relaxed, less fatigued teacher. You will become a teacher who gets praise from students, parents and administrators for your well-managed classroom involving students in higher level thinking skills. The activities I will share with you will also *reduce* your planning and paper correcting time.

Because I am writing this book as if I were talking to you, there will be places where I take liberties with classical writing rules. CAPITAL LETTERS mean I am making an important statement and raising my voice, raising my eyebrows and opening my eyes wider (scary huh?). Besides using *italics* for specific titles, I will also use *italicized words* to get an extra oomph of emphasis. I will also use words (like oomph) that one would not usually see in an instruction book. I will even make up some words! I'm trying to make the text easy to read and friendly to the mind's "ear." For me, the language of text books puts me to sleep in about five pages. I want you to get involved in the conversations of this book and suddenly realize you have read twenty pages! So, if you are an English teacher, please give me lots of flexibility. I hope you will make notes in the margins, use post-its to mark special pages and dog-ear the pages. USE THIS BOOK TO INCREASE STUDENT RESPONSIBILITY AND REDUCE TEACHER FATIGUE.

You will recognize some of the ideas presented here as originating from others. I have not *created* all the ideas in this book, but I have collected others' ideas with education in mind. I am also skilled at modifying collected ideas into lesson plans. I will certainly give credit, if I know where the idea came from. However, many of the ideas come from over 30 years of teaching, lots of learning theory classes and years of attending conferences. So any lapse in giving credit to others is unintentional.

Before we get too far, I would like to share with you a little of how I got motivated to create *Teaching Smarter*. Like most people, I changed my teaching approach because of a personal professional crisis. After all, the only person who *really* likes change is a wet baby. Change takes effort, and why would one want to work harder if what they are currently doing is working OK? (Unless, of course, someone like *me* comes along and says "You can do as good a job—or better—with LESS STRESS. But, I didn't know anyone like that. All I kept hearing was "We have to change." And all the ideas for change seemed like *more* work for the teacher!)

I was teaching at a high school where we had decided to aggressively pursue systemic change. We were going to be LEADERS. The good news was, we were nationally recognized for excellence. The bad news was, there were *lots* of meetings. Teams met during planning times (which were scheduled to be in common). Teams met before school and after school. We were creating curriculum and trying to change the way we worked with students while continuing to work a full teaching day. (This effort is sometimes referred to as changing a car's tire—while it continues to travel down the road at 55 miles an hour.) The integrated effort involved only three of my six classes. All paper correcting and personal planning for classes not involved in the team effort was done in my "spare time." Now, that might be OK for one year of "development." However, every year teachers would leave. We were so "cutting edge" that now we were not only creating new curriculum AND teaching "regular" classes, we were also in a constant training phase for the new people!

I began to have stress headaches, tense muscles, sleepless nights. When I had severe chest pains and wore a heart monitor for a week, I decided I HAD to change the way I was teaching. Two 911 calls later, due to shortness of breath, I truly felt teaching in the way I currently was could possibly kill me. (I mean, how many messages does one's body need to send?) There *must* be something better than "trying harder" and working longer.

I changed districts, not because my problems were the fault of the district, but because I knew it would be easier to totally change the way I do business in my classroom if I was in a new environment. It was hard to leave the place where I had worked for nine years. I was friends with some very fine teachers.

However, if I were on a cruise ship going to Spain, and I wanted to go to Greece, it wouldn't make sense for me to make a lot of noise and splash my oars in the water. The ship would *still* go to Spain! I *needed* to change ships at the next port of call. I needed to find a ship that was going the direction of Greece. Now, this little story may seem obvious, but there are people on staffs who bitterly complain about what is going on at a particular school, but they never consider going to a different school!

The entire next summer I did a research project on how I could do business differently in my classroom. I love teaching. I didn't want to leave the profession. I had a solid background in learning theory. Besides my master's degree, I had over 90 additional credits in learning theory. Theory knowledge was *not* the problem! Where else could I look for ideas? Then I thought about taking seminars from the business world. What techniques were being used by the business world to successfully manage people? I took classes like "How to manage difficult people," "How to handle paper work" and "How to make a good presentation." After all, we manage people every day. We have lots of paper work to manage. We have time management problems. We encounter "difficult" people.

Also, I took David Langford's *Quality Learning Seminar*. This course is based on Dr. Deming's "Total Quality Management" theories. Dr. Deming is the man who went to Japan in the late 1940's and helped guide the "Total Quality Management" of Japanese car manufacturing. We all know how successful that was! Then Dr. Deming came back to the U.S. and helped some of the very same businesses that had rejected him previously. "Quality Management" is now a big part of many large companies including Kellogg, Motorola, IBM, Ford, Chrysler, Starbucks Coffee and the Boeing Company.

Perhaps, I thought, business management and leadership techniques would give me some new ideas for classroom management. One of the *Quality Learning Seminar* ideas is called "Imagineering." One tries to imagine the perfect solution or environment, with no limits on money or time. What would the perfect condition be? Here is an imagineered list of my ideas for a perfect classroom:

- students take responsibility and pride in their work
- students are motivated to do quality work
- there are very few behavior problems
- disruptors are not supported by their peers
- I start each class relaxed and well planned
- paper work does not consume me
- students are generally happy
- I can go home within 45 minutes of the last bell
- I leave and the next day is fully planned
- I go home at night with the energy to run a few errands, have quality time with my family, and maybe even mow the lawn!

So, the frustration and health problems led to a motivation for change. I did the research. I imagineered. I changed my place of work so I could work differently. I wondered, "Will I be successful?" If not, I had decided to leave teaching knowing I had done everything I could to stay in the profession I loved *and* stay healthy. It took three years of trying, modifying, evaluating, and retrying. Now I'm in better health, I'm in my imagineered classroom and I love teaching again! Sure, I still have one of *those days* every now and then—but rarely.

The Ninth Grade Story

Let me share just one more story with you before we get to the "nuts and bolts" of *Teaching Smarter*. In the new district I went to, I was hired to teach earth science to ninth grade students at a four year high school where we had 103 minute class periods. We had periods 1, 2, 3 one day and periods 4, 5, 6 the next day (a rotating 6 period day). However, my new district was a growing community. The current high school could no longer house all students. Soooo, half the ninth graders went on to high school and half *stayed* at the junior high. The method of choice was by application. Those students who filled in the paperwork, and got it in on time, would attend the high school. Although it seemed a good idea at the time, this process left the junior high site with students who did not fill out paperwork, or couldn't get it in on time, or students who were new to the district. There was a lot of anger from students who had been looking forward to "gettin outta here" and now would spend another year at the junior high site. There was a significant amount of negative student leadership. As often happens when the powerless feel anger towards a system, we had many incidences of vandalism and behavior problems.

One major problem involved lunchroom behavior. Students would throw food, leave garbage on the floor and tables, sneak outside to stomp the small catsup envelopes on floors and on walls. There was more, but you get the idea. The response from administration was to increase control. (This is known as "The beatings will continue until morale improves" method.) We had a total of six teachers and administrators standing at lunchroom doors and roving through the lunchroom. Still, there is no way even six adults can force good behavior from 250 students. The final straw was the administrative threat of a lock-down lunch, rather like a jail lunch.

Students would enter the lunch room, the doors would be locked and a teacher would be at every door. Students would remain in the lunch room until it was time to go to class. Students, of course, threatened to riot. Because the situation was sooo bad, my principal was willing to allow me a chance to apply the ideas of *Teaching Smarter* to reach a possible solution.

Since my class was a required course, I saw every ninth grade student at the junior high site. By using methods you will learn later in this book, I helped students see how they could change the system from within. If most of the people in a system want change, there are ways to motivate change that do not involve violence. (Talk about a good life skill to have!) I helped *students* decide "What behaviors are reasonable to expect in order for ninth grade students to have unstructured lunch?" *Students* then developed a consequences chart for those who did not follow the students' rules. At a staff meeting, *students* presented their commitments and the data that led to the commitments. We had twelve representatives and six large sheets of butcher paper full of the supporting data. The staff was in awe! (See *figure 1-1* at the end of this chapter for a summary of the behavior commitments, and for the student-developed consequences for lack of compliance. I will teach you how to do this technique in Part II.)

On a humorous note, I had instructed the presenting students to dress up for the staff meeting. "After all," I said, "if you want teachers to consider you in a different light, you need to look more grown up than you do on a daily basis in the classroom." Now, I was thinking business attire, but I guess I didn't make that clear because some of the girls came in looking like they were dressed up for a prom! Ah yes, we all live and learn! (Also, it reminded me how young and naïve ninth graders really are.)

In most systems the 10% suboptimizers control the rules developed by the system. (Suboptimizers are people who keep a system from working at its best—more on this later.) We make rules to govern the system in response to people who break the assumed code of conduct. So, we make rules for the 100% based on the actions of 10%. That leaves 90% of the people dealing with rules they never helped cause and which they consider unnecessary! With the *Teaching Smarter* technique, the 90% get to make the rules. This is a profound change. It puts the majority of people, who always were willing to cooperate, in charge.

In the junior high case, the 90+% students took charge and it was *their* rules made up for *their* lunch time. Suddenly, the suboptimizers were no longer the "hero rebel" acting out against the adult rule makers. There was no longer support for throwing tater tots or tossing garbage around. (When the student committee made their presentation to classrooms for the consequences resulting from not following the student rules for lunch room conduct, one of the students remarked, "That's too harsh!" A student committee member replied, "Then don't throw taters—Tater Tot Tad!" I had always suspected it was him!)

The student plan was voted on and accepted by staff. The supervision number quickly went to two adults, and sometimes one. Students left the lunchroom clean. The agreement charts hung on the lunchroom wall from January to June. In June I removed the charts and there was not one food stain or graffiti mark on them! This was truly *systemic change.*

Initially, there were two lunch periods at the school. The second lunch period had both eighth and ninth grade students in it. Once empowered, the students wanted to design a lunch schedule where ninth graders would have a lunch period strictly for ninth graders. The principal said, "We will need a third lunch next year due to enrollment. So, why not. I was dreading the meeting time needed to structure the scheduling. If the kids can do it, more power to them!" I gave them the number of minutes needed for class, passing time and for lunch. Students came up with *three* plans, and presented them to the principal. He accepted one and the ninth graders had their own lunch period for the last three months of school. Now they were "on a roll!"

The students then gathered and presented data to the district nutrition specialist, who cooperated with their suggestions and ordered more lunches with foods students liked. (Please see *figures 1-2* through *1-5* at the end of the chapter for copies of *some* of the letters students wrote at the end of the ninth grade year.)

This was an incredible transformation! Students moved the perception from "You gotta watch these kids every second." to "This is one of the best lunch groups I have ever seen!" I knew *Teaching Smarter* was a winner! After all, what is it *all* adolescents want? Control over the decisions that concern them. They are already making profound decisions about whether or not to have sex, whether or not to drink or do drugs, and whether or not to drive responsibly. Why shouldn't we involve them in important decisions about school? What *Teaching Smarter* does is give the teacher a structure for helping students make decisions in an orderly and concise way.

In June of that year I received "Teacher of the Year from the PTA." This was the first time a teacher new to the district had received the honor. SO, THIS "STUFF" REALLY DOES WORK!

Teaching Smarter is created

My husband said "Sandy, you have lightning in a bottle. You *must* share these ideas with other teachers." I was reluctant. After all, I do not have a Ph.D. "But Sandy," he replied, " you *do* have P.O.E.—Plenty Of Experience. What would *you* have given as a new or struggling teacher to have someone with successful classroom management experience share their techniques with you?"

So, I began to teach some workshops. The response was overwhelming! People came up to me and said things like, "I learned more from you in a few hours than I learned in all my college experiences!" or "I can't believe how much more organized and relaxed I am, and it's so easy!" or (the one that still gives me goose bumps—because I remember what it feels like) "Thank you so much for your ideas. Now I am sleeping through the night." Comments like these have given me the encouragement I needed for doing my best to share ideas. It is worth all the hard work if the ideas will help others ease the heavy load that is teaching.

Once I gained my confidence in giving workshops, my husband said, "Sandy, you have to write a book." Now isn't *he* just the fine one with good ideas of how I can work harder! I have to admit though, he does have good ideas. So here I am writing a book. Once again I have my doubts. After all I am a math and science person. Writing and literature are not my strong suit. But the message is a good one, and maybe if I try to write like I would talk to you, I can get the message across in a readable manner?

Please remember, this will be a *buffet of ideas*. Just like a buffet, some ideas you will want to take back to your classes and use right away, just as they are presented. Other ideas you may want to *season* to better fit your teaching style or situation. A few ideas you may say, "Nope, not for me." (Perhaps you don't like the idea, or you have a classroom *receipe* of your own that better fits a particular task.)

If you, my dear colleague, get even *one* good idea from this book which results in more responsible students and/or a less fatigued you—I will feel the effort to write this book was worth it.

Good Luck—and now let's get to it!

Figure 1-1

List of the ninth grade lunch room
Behavior Contract headings

(Remember, these are the *category headings* developed after the Affinity Diagram process of data gathering—more about this process in Chapter 10.)

Teacher generated question:
"What behaviors are reasonable to expect so ninth grade students can have open lunch?"

Student developed categories
Food in right places, No smoking, Trash in right places, Stay on the first floor, Appropriate level of supervision, Respect (both ways), Good behavior, No stereotyping, Trust (both ways)

"Consequences for Inappropriate Lunch Room Behavior"

(*Student developed* consequences for noncompliance with the *student generated* Behavior Contract for lunch room behavior.)

Strike 1 Read commitment statements out loud (to a lunch room supervisor)
Strike 2 Copy the rules *5* times during a *before* school time
Strike 3 Clean up in the lunch room for at least 15 minutes of *your* lunch time for ONE WEEK
Strike 4 Parent phone call and two weeks of closed lunch for that person (stay in seat, no talking, eat in in-school suspension room)
Strike 5 Parent phone call and two Saturday School days and/or four weeks of closed lunch
Strike 6 Closed lunch for the rest of the year

* Enlarging Tip:
To achieve an 8$^{1}/_{2}$"x11" copy of the samples shown in all figures, set the machine to enlarge 175%.

Figure 1-2

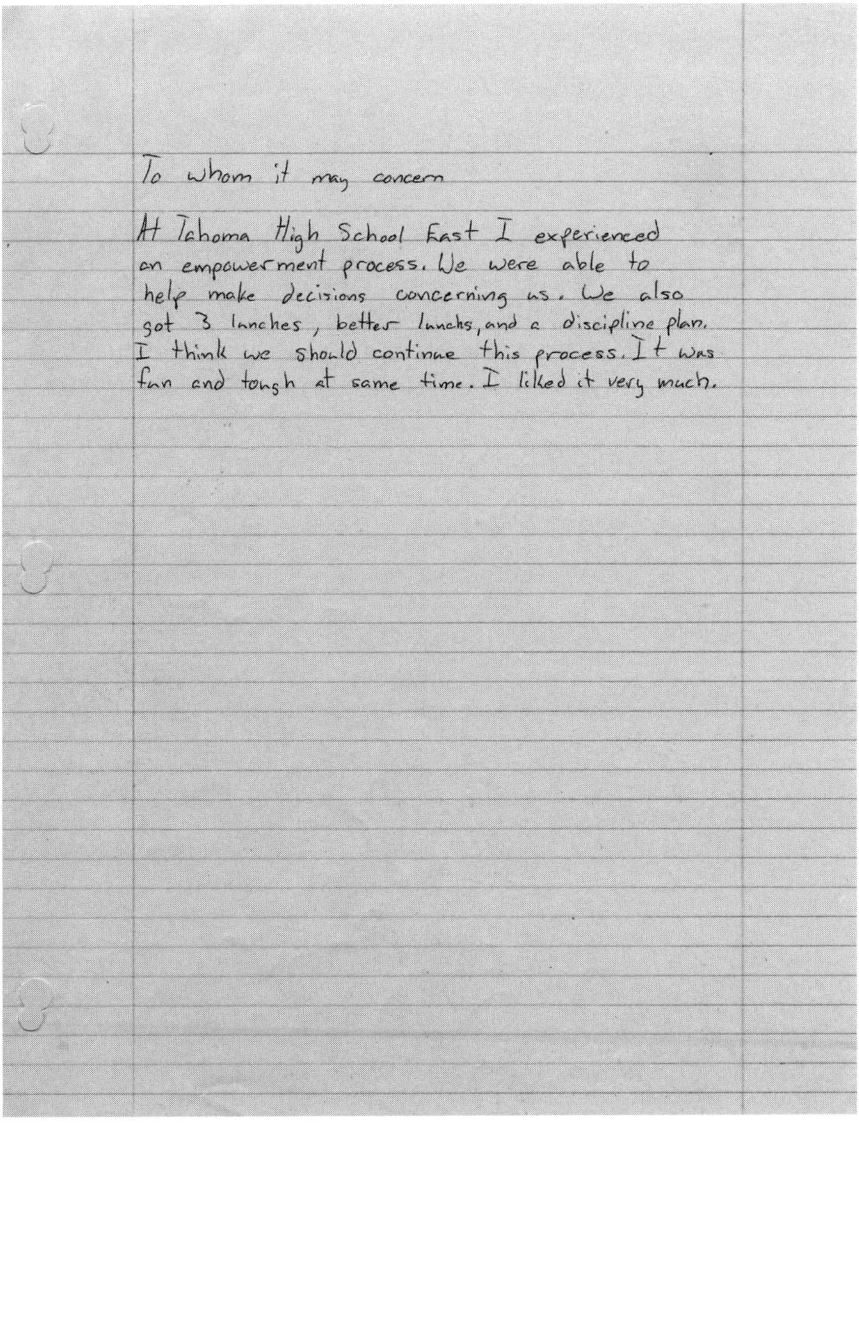

To whom it may concern

At Tahoma High School East I experienced an empowerment process. We were able to help make decisions concerning us. We also got 3 lunches, better lunchs, and a discipline plan. I think we should continue this process. It was fun and tough at same time. I liked it very much.

Figure 1-3

to whom it may concein

as a nineth grade student I have been affect by Mrs. Labelles empowerment program. I think it is great. It gave me the feeling of being important. And not just a student but someone with a voice.

I think if I was a teacher I would definetly use the empowerment program. It gave me a better relatienship w/ the teacher because it should me she really cared about what the students really wanted

Figure 1-4

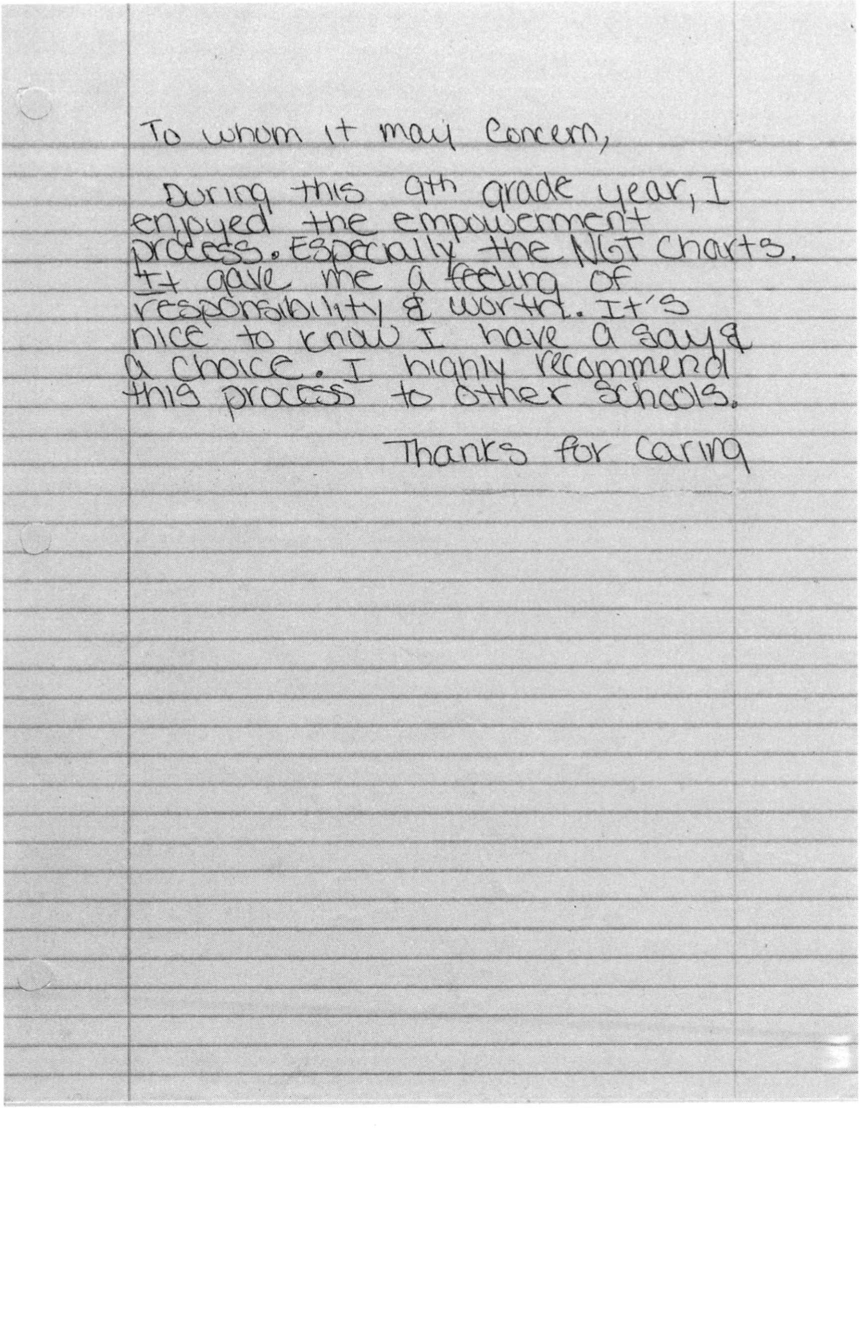

To whom it may Concern,

During this 9th grade year, I enjoyed the empowerment process. Especially the NGT Charts. It gave me a feeling of responsibility & worth. It's nice to know I have a say & a choice. I highly recommend this process to other Schools.

Thanks for Caring

Figure 1-5

To Whom it may Concern,

As an 9th grade student who has been envolved in the empowerment process I think it has helped me alot. It has shown me that my voice and opion is important. I can help to solve the problem instead of just complaining.

CHAPTER 2

How to value time

Do the best job you can in the time that you have. Like most good advice, I have found this suggestion hard for most of us to follow. It has been my experience that teachers have no problem with the first part, "Do the best job you can." Where we *do* have problems is with the second part "in the time that you have." We have high quality standards for our work. When we are not getting the response we feel we should, *we* work harder. We steal sleep time and come in earlier, or we stay later and rob from family or personal time. Or, we take work home. Working *harder* is not the answer, working *smarter* is.

I want to share with you some of the easy-to-implement techniques for managing paperwork and planning for lessons. Then we will move into exactly how one can structure *Teaching Smarter* and move teachers and students into the environment of the new century. Together, we will structure an environment of mutually beneficial cooperation. By using *Teaching Smarter* ideas you will have a classroom where students function more willingly at a higher level of thought and responsibility. You will have a classroom where you feel more comfortable as the *manager* of learning.

GOAL: STUDENTS WILL BE ACTIVELY ON TASK WITHIN ONE MINUTE OF THE START OF CLASS, THE TEACHER WILL BE RELAXED, ABLE TO TAKE ROLL AND PREPARE FOR INSTRUCTION WITHOUT INTERRUPTION FOR *AT LEAST* THREE MINUTES.

I know, three minutes does not sound like much time. I want you to try this exercise, look at a watch or clock with a second hand. When the second hand moves to 12, I want you to close your eyes and "feel" how long one minute is. Now, no fair counting or using any other pacing technique, just "feel" one minute's worth of time. If you are like most teachers, you will open your eyes somewhere around 35 to 45 seconds. As teachers we have a pretty good sense of time. (If you are like me, I "felt" one minute of time, then thought "I'll give it a little more, well maybe a little more, surely it's been one minute by now!" I was at 45 seconds.) Most adults who are not in teaching open their eyes somewhere around 25 to 35 seconds. You see, we have all been conditioned that one minute is not much time. Actually, it is enough time to get quite a bit done. Think about how much money is paid for *one minute* of advertising time during the Super Bowl!

OK, here's how you can get students on task within one minute of the class start time. I have used this technique with many different types of students and abilities for many years. It works!

FIRST, if we want students to value the start time, WE must value it by paying attention to it. In my classroom I have a radio playing soft jazz during class change time (it seems to calm the students down as they transition from "friend time" to "class time"). Near the door, on a table or counter, are the papers they need to pick up for the day. It is *their* responsibility to get their papers on the way to their seat. At one minute before start time I announce "One minute until class begins." If I am visiting with a student or adult, I simply ask them to excuse me while I start class, and I'll be right back with them—so far no one has ever objected, and administrators are impressed! I then announce "Thirty seconds until class starts."

At ten seconds until class begins, I turn off the radio and announce "Ten seconds until class starts." At the start time, the overhead goes on and there is a question for students to copy and answer within the first five minutes of class.

Any student who enters class when the music is off and the overhead is on, knows they are tardy. This eliminates the "AM I TARDY?" loudly said as the attention seeker enters the room and disrupts the class.

This routine is done EVERY DAY. I actually have young people from other classes crowded around my door visiting with my students right before the bell rings. You see, *everyone* knows this class starts on time. Friends can afford to visit at my doorway until the bell rings because they know their teacher runs late in starting. Being on time is an important school-to-work skill, but students need to see it modeled by their leader. They also need a *personal* reason for why it is important to them *today* to be on time.

Early Work

The question students copy and answer is called "Early Work" and they know it will be on the overhead or board EVERY DAY. Do not uncover the question until class begins.

Students know they have the first five minutes of class to get paper, pencil, and notes out—copy the question- write the answer—and turn the paper into the collection box. The activity is worth up to five points each day. Now, this is not a "stump the stars" or a test quality question or an essay question. This is a "structured for success" *long* question and *short* answer based on something learned last class session.

Keep in mind the station that everyone likes to listen to is station WIIFM (**W**hat's **I**n **I**t **F**or **M**e?). In the past, I played WIIFM in mono, what's in it for my students, not necessarily for me (that seemed somehow selfish). IT IS NOT SELFISH TO CONSIDER YOURSELF! (Remember, all capitals is the only way in print I can raise my voice and my eyebrows!) The Early Work technique is WIIFM in stereo. The students get an easy shot at five points and the teacher gets up to five minutes of peace to do "administrivia" (one of those made-up words) like attendance, admits and lesson set up. You might even get a few seconds to take a deep breath while students finish the Early Work! Everybody wins, and that's great—and that's a major focus of *Teaching Smarter.*

THE STUDENTS DON'T MIND A CLASS THAT STARTS THE SAME WAY EVERY DAY. In fact 99% of them really like it. Remember, they have other teachers with different expectations every day. They have more variety in their day than they need. It's OK to be consistent!

Part of "responsibility moving-overmanship" (another made-up word) is structuring your classroom to provide the opportunity for students to take action in their own behalf. Do not collect the papers yourself. If the teacher collects papers and a paper is not collected, who can be blamed? That's right, "The teacher didn't collect my paper." Instead, use a Rubbermaid wash tub. They come in different colors, they are durable, and they are 9" x 12" on the bottom (perfect for notebook papers). I even put a Teddy Bear next to the tub. That's right, a Teddy Bear. Students almost never miss the direction, "Put your paper in the green box by the Teddy Bear." *Now,* whose fault is it if the paper is not turned in?

One of my workshop participants was having trouble getting students to buy in to the five minute limit on Early Work. Her solution? Stand by the box, announce when it had been four minutes and thirty seconds, forty seconds, fifty seconds, FIVE MINUTES. At five minutes, she made a big show of taking the papers that were in the box, stacking them together and putting a staple through them. She then returned the stapled stack to the box.

Could students still put Early Work in the box? Yes, they just lost a point for being late. Took about three times and the problem was solved! Great Job! She supported the ability of students to get some points, but also rewarded the students who were on time.

Don't forget, the PURPOSE of the Early Work is to have students in their seats and working within one minute of the bell to start class. The task is to be finished within five minutes so we can all move on to the first lesson of the day. Students should be motivated to be on time for Early Work and ready to learn by five minutes into the class period.

What about correction? The bad news is, you need to correct Early Work every day. Don't despair my friend, it only takes about 30 to 45 seconds per class of 30 to correct. The slow-down is writing the five point score on the paper! If it takes you a minute or more to correct a class set—review the question technique of LONG question and SHORT answer.

Here is a sample question and answer from one of my Earth Science classes.

- What were the three types of plate boundaries we learned about in class last time? (hint: look in your notes)
- Answer: Subduction, Transverse, Divergent

See, I even tell them where to look for the answer! Remember, the PURPOSE of Early Work is to have students on task within one minute of the bell ringing and for you to have some time for "administrivia" with maybe a moment to take a deep breath. The students buy in because they can easily earn five points.

When I first began to use Early Work, I did not realize the strong positive impact five points a day could have. I'll never forget this one young man. He used Kool-Aid and alcohol to color his hair various brilliant colors. He had a "hard" and cocky exterior with tattoos and numerous body piercings. He was not an academically successful student. One day he came into class a little early (a rare occurrence) before the other students were in the class. He picked up his Early Work and said softly, "Wow, three perfect scores in a row…I've never had three perfect scores in a row in anything…Huh." Then he sauntered over to his desk, put his stuff down and went out in the hallway to visit with his buddies.

During this event, I was sitting at my desk and grading papers. He never looked at me. After all, he was talking to himself. I felt like I had just glimpsed the soft inside underneath the hard exterior of this young man. He was 17 years old and in awe that he had earned 3-in-a-row perfect scores. Some of the young people we work with have experienced so much failure in school. An every day positive pump has incredible power. EVERYBODY likes to be successful!

Just one more short story regarding the power of the positive pump. After one of my seminars, a teacher came up to me and said, "I've been teaching for 26 years. When you started talking about Early Work I thought, 'Big deal, I've been doing that for years.' But after your story about the 17 year old young man I realized, 'Oh my goodness, I've been starting each class with *failure!'* You see, I was starting each class with a short task I knew they needed to improve on. Then I was dismayed with how each class seemed to start with unhappy students who were unwilling to try when I gave the new lesson. It's so obvious, but I never saw it!" Later that week, the teacher called me to say how that one simple change (moving from a negative reminder to a positive pump) had changed the attitude of the class significantly. Sometimes it's the *small* change that can make *so much difference* in the way our class runs!

When I correct Early Work, do I read every question? No, I can tell with a glance if students have copied the whole question. You will probably have a few students who will attempt to shorten the question. They can certainly do that—but "it'll cost ya" a point or two for not following directions.

I do not put the Early Work score in the grade book each day—good grief that would be *way* too much work! I wait until we have completed ten questions for a total of fifty points. At that time I give each student a cover sheet (see *figure 2-1* and *2-2* at the end of the chapter for a blank cover sheet and for a sample model sheet I might have on the overhead). Students are asked to look at each of their past Early Works and think of three or four words to describe the question. (The more times a student interacts with data, the more likely it will be learned.) These titles are entered on the cover sheet. Students then tally up their scores and enter a total on the cover sheet. (By tallying up the scores, students are able to revisit the fact that they earned a lot of good scores in your class; this builds a positive mind set towards your class.) They then staple the work to the cover sheet and turn the packet in to the green box by the Teddy Bear. I correct by adding up the scores I see on their *daily* work sheet and compare it to the total score they recorded on the cover sheet. If I agree with their score, I circle it in a colored felt tip pen on the cover sheet. If I do not agree with their tally, I simply put the new score on the cover sheet in felt tip pen. THEN I enter the scores in the grade book. The whole check, add and enter process takes about ten minutes per class of thirty. The new set of Early Work begins the next class day with a clean sheet of notebook paper (whether or not the packets are graded and returned).

One of the questions that always comes up in my workshops is "What about students who are absent?" Every day we can count on about a 10% absentee rate in most classes. Wouldn't it be great if all students could be in class every day? However, that is not the reality we deal with. Here is how I handle it. First, I design it so I look like the hero. I say, "Early Work is set up to have students on time and on task within one minute of the class start time. Since you were not here, some people would say you can not get any points. However, I don't think that is right, so I will meet you half way. That means you could earn half the points, or up to 2½ of the 5 points. Then I will round in *your* favor and give you the possibility of earning three points. You may either write the word 'absent' and the date, or you may want to copy the date, question and answer from someone else's paper (since Early Work questions often end up on tests). Either way you can earn up to three points." Whenever possible, I find it is best to give people a choice, it makes them feel more in control of their life.

I realize in some school systems there is a rule that we must provide full points for make up work missed during an excused absence. If that is the case at your school, just require that they write "absent" and then copy the question and answer if they want the 5 points. (See *figure 2-3* and *2-4* at the end of this chapter for samples of students' daily Early Work papers and filled in Early Work cover sheets)

Briefly, let's recap how we can have students on task within one minute of the class start time.

1. Have music playing during class break time.
2. Put papers on a table or counter near the entrance door for students to pick up their work before class begins (responsibility moving-overmanship).
3. Count down for the beginning of class.
4. Turn off the radio ten seconds before class starts.
5. Turn on the overhead when class begins.
6. Have an Early Work question on the overhead.
7. Give students five minutes to copy the question, answer the question and turn the paper into the collection box.
8. If necessary, have a system for rewarding those who get their paper in the box within the five minute time frame. (Remember the staple together trick?)

When do I give the first Early Work? During the first day of class, or the first day I begin the *Teaching Smarter* techniques. I model on the overhead EXACTLY how the paper should be set up. I also model how the class will begin from now on. The second day of class the students are ready to pick up their papers and do the Early Work within the first five minutes.

In order to change a habit, it takes at least 20 repetitions. BE VERY CONSISTENT FOR 20 DAYS before expecting the students and yourself to be on automatic response for the Early Work habit. Twenty working days is about one month.

Never forget to model, model, model expectations for students. One teacher's quality expectations are *not* the same as the next. We cannot expect students to spend time on quality if we do not. One of my relatives used to say, "Do as I say, not as I do. You'll understand when you get older." Although I have to admit to being "older," I still do not agree with that statement. We MUST model what we want from our young people, because I firmly believe that "actions speak louder than words."

For example, we may *say* it is important to get to class on time and be ready to work. However if we, as teachers, do not get to class on time, or worse yet, if we are in class, but are *not* prepared and *do not* start class on time, why would students think it really IS important to be in class and prepared on time? At one of my schools, some of the very people who wanted the strictest rules for tardy policies, were the same ones who were late to staff meetings! My friends, we cannot afford to do that. It undermines our validity with our students. WE MUST ADHERE TO THE SAME STANDARDS WE EXPECT OF OUR STUDENTS! If I have five minutes to leave one classroom, travel from one side of the campus to the other and set up for the next class, I may not be ready when the bell rings. In this case I modify my student expectations in a consistent manner. For example, I may say to them, "I expect you at the door by the class start time. I will give you two extra minutes to be ready for Early Work, since I may not get here until the bell rings."

I KNOW this class start model will work for an entire school because I had the honor of working as a consultant with an entire high school staff. The Early Work was one of their favorite ideas. Some staff members had already been using a class start idea (like journals or paragraph entries). These activities are usually not Early Work because of the time it takes for students to complete them, and because students do not receive a "positive point pump" EVERY DAY. However, the LONG question and SHORT answer task plays WIIFM in stereo so sweetly! The principal remarked that the biggest difference in class start atmosphere was observed in classrooms with several "at risk" students. This same school district was beginning the next year with a new superintendent. The principal told me it was great to brag "At our school students are on task within one minute of the bell ringing."

IT'S EASY, IT WORKS, TRY IT, YOU'LL LIKE IT!!

Figure 2-1

Sample cover sheet for the Early Work packets (after 10 days)

Name ______________________ Period __________

GRADE RECORD

Subject: ______________

DATE	TOPIC	SCORE
	TOTAL	

Figure 2-2

What I put on the overhead the day we collect Early Work packets.

Name ______________________ Period __________

GRADE RECORD

Subject: Earth Science

DATE	TOPIC	SCORE
10/6	U.S. Hurricanes	/5
10/8	Tornado warning	/5
10/12	How many thunderstorms	/5
10/14		/5
10/16		/5
10/20		/5
10/22		/5
10/26		/5
10/28		/5
10/30		/5
	TOTAL	/50

Extra Credit =

Total

I give them the first three topics, they do the rest. Remember, this is a class that meets every other day.

Figure 2-3

Extra Credit Stamps

Early work

First & Last Name
E. Science P.2
Oct. 6, 1998

1) When do U.S. Hurricanes happen most often?

late summer & early fall 5

2) What do we call it when a Tornado has been seen and people need to get prepared?

Tornado warning 5

Student daily Early Work Sheet

3) How many thunder storm occur in a day

44,000. 3

4) What is the Temprature range -4- Seattle on Sept. 30th

20. 5

5. What 2 things are the major elements of Climate?

5 Temprature & precipitation.

#7, 8, 9, 10 were on the back

6. Tell the 4 things that influence Climate Temp 5

Latitude, altitude, large bodies of water, ocean currents.

Figure 2-3b

⑦ Tell the three ways that heat is transferred through the atmosphere.
Suns radiation surface of the air, conduction & Carried aloft by convection
5
⑧ Tell the three main ways climate changes naturally.
5
Glaciers, plate Tectonics, ocean currents.
⑨ Tell the 4 major ways humans cause climate change
3
microclimate, fossil fuels
Gulf war, Carbon Dioxide
⑩ Tell the Due date for on-time weather Data Labs
Oct. 28
5

Figure 2-4

Name First and Last Name Period # 2

Subject: Earth Science GRADE RECORD

DATE	TOPIC	SCORE
10/6	US Hurricanes.	5/5
10/8	Tornado warning	5/5
10/12	How many thunderstorms.	3/5
10/14	Temp. for Seattle on Sept. 30	5/5
10/16	2 major elements of climate.	5/5
10/20	4 things that influence temp.	5/5
10/22	3 ways heat is transferred	5/5
10/26	3 ways climate changes	5/5
10/28	4 ways humans change climate	3/5
10/30	Due Date for Weather lab	5/5
	TOTAL	46/50

Extra Credit = 10

Total = 56/50

Student cover sheet that is stapled on top of daily Early Work Sheet.

CHAPTER 3

How to Manage Time Better

How to get students' cooperative attention within 30 seconds or less

Many times I have watched as a teacher asks for students' attention, waits until *almost* all students have responded, and then begins to give instructions. Please know that a student who has not given you their attention when you asked for it, will not give you any better attention once you begin to talk. More often, some students will give a moment of attention, then begin to talk as soon as the teacher talks!

I tried many different methods before hitting on the one I'm going to share with you now. HERE'S HOW WE CAN ACHIEVE 100% ATTENTION FROM STUDENTS WITHOUT RAISING OUR VOICE OR GETTING MAD.

By now students are used to the time count down for class to start. I share with them that there are times when I will need to ask for the attention of the entire class. Since I may be interrupting their conversation, I want to respect their need to finish their sentences before giving me attention. (Students appreciate this respectful manner.) Therefore, I will say, "I need your attention in 30 seconds. I need no talking and eyes up here (yes, we need to be THAT SPECIFIC) in 20 seconds, in 10, 5, now." Usually, that is enough. If there are still students who have not given you the asked for attention, I say, "Oh no, some people are still talking." Then after 5 seconds I write on the overhead +5, after 10 seconds +10 etc. until *all* students have given me the asked for 100% attention. This time written on the overhead is served after the class ending time. Students are required to sit silently at their assigned seats until the entire time is served. If anyone talks, we start the time over again. There is very little that students value more than the time after class is over.

Now, this only really works well if the "door swings both ways." By this I mean, if you ask for students' attention in 30 seconds and everyone is quiet with eyes on you in 20 seconds, then 10 seconds comes *off* the time to serve. The PURPOSE of this activity is to build peer support for doing as the teacher asks. In elementary school I was able to get attention because "teacher said." In secondary schools, I have found WIIFM must be playing for students before I can count on cooperation. Students will almost always ask, "Can we earn time to go early?" This is where I help them understand that I have bosses too. I usually say something like, "I would love to offer you that option, however, my boss has specifically told the teachers that we are to keep students in class until the appointed time." It is amazing how many students seem to think that, as a teacher, we get to make *all* the rules!

In my workshops, teachers sometimes ask, "Don't you run the risk of making students late to their next class?" In using this method for several years, the longest time I have ever had a class stay is 55 seconds. The longest 55 seconds of their lives, I'm sure! Remember, YOU have a lot of control over the time to be served. It really only takes about 10 seconds to have students' attention, if they are motivated. The peer group is very motivated to negatively reinforce the talkers, if after-class time is on the line. With this method it is OK to support the teacher. After all, no one wants to stay extra time.

I have to admit to a smallness in my personality. If a class has been particularly rude and uncooperative, I do exact a certain amount of pleasure from seeing them "suffer" after the bell has rung and they are sitting in their seats silently while their friends are out in the halls. It helps to relieve my anxiety and stress that was built up during the period. That way I can face the next class in a better mood. So much for any image I may have had as the "classroom management expert" who never gets mad or never wants to "get even!" Hey, I'm human, and if it helps me face my next class without "baggage" from the previous class, I think it's OK.

One other question I sometimes get from teachers in my workshops is, "What about students who complain that it is unfair for the whole class to serve time? How do you answer that?" I set the scene as I explain this method for the first time. I share with students, "We are working together to get the best quality learning we can. I do not want to be the CONTROLLING BOSS, I am the facilitator of learning and I need your help. We all work together. I need the whole class team working together, so when I give 30 seconds for 100% attention, I need your help to make it happen. Do not allow the suboptimizers to keep us after class so they can get attention." This method gives the 90+% a way to help you, without being *apple polishers*. The student support we can get when their peers support the system is wonderful!

Give it a try. I have found that the more immature the class is, the better this method works. In my physics classes, I can simply ask for attention. Most other classes I need to use this technique for at least a few times. In fact, my traditionally most-difficult-to-manage classes respond very positively to this technique. THE KIDS ARE TIRED OF SUBOPTIMIZERS RULING THE SYSTEM!

How to reduce your planning time

I have found a way to handle three or four preparation responsibilities while spending much less time than I used to. I call it the "Skeleton Schedule." The name is based on the idea that humans have very similar skeletons, but we do not all look alike from the outside observers point of view.

This technique requires a few sheets of overhead plastic, some permanent markers and some erasable felt tip pens. At the top of the plastic I write in permanent pen, "Welcome to (whatever class it is)." Just below that line I write the word "Date" (this really comes in handy for the "what day is it" question I used to get several times each period). The next line says "Early Work." This is followed by about a four or five inch space. Then I write the word "Schedule." The rest of the page is left blank (See *figure 3-1* at the end of this chapter for a sample). I make two copies of this plastic for each preparation period I have. This plastic sheet, filled out in erasable pen, is the first thing students see EVERY DAY as the class period begins (See *figure 3-2* at the end of this chapter for a sample). Students reflect that they like knowing what is on the schedule each day. It lets them know there is a plan and a purpose to the class time. It's amazing how many students think we come in and just "wing it." When students see the skeleton schedule they also know what is expected of them during this period of time. Station WIIFM is playing in stereo because I do not have to remember what I planned, and in what order I planned to present it. I simply look at the plastic. This was really handy one year when I was teaching the oceanography part of earth science at the same time I was teaching a semester long oceanography class. The classes were very similar, but never in the same place at the same time. It would have been *so* easy to teach the wrong lesson, the classes were sooo similar. I found myself referring to the "Skeleton Schedule" many times each period.

The make-up of the schedule follows a skeleton plan as well. First, we do Early Work. Then while students are "fresh" we do an individually focused activity (like read, or write, or take notes from teacher lecture). This lesson is followed by some sort of group activity. The class ends with some type of individual participation activity (like correct a paper, watch a video or work on a word puzzle). Then there is the consistent closure, and students leave the class.

Just as human beings have the same basic skeletons, but do not look exactly alike, my lessons have a skeleton plan, but do not appear to be boringly alike. This method is particularly handy when I have multiple preps. I can pick a quiet time and fill out the plastic sheets with erasable pen. That way modifications are easy, but I still have a general idea of what I want to do for each class.

How to increase the quality of students' work *and* decrease your paper correction time.

I struggled and struggled with, "How can I get my students to produce the quality job I know they are capable of?" The same student who acted so immaturely in my class, could be seen at their place of work acting quite maturely and responsibly. "What was I doing or not doing?" I came to the conclusion that station WIIFM must be playing so softly for them, they couldn't hear it in my class! Perhaps I needed to make it REALLY obvious how important it was to them *right now* to do a quality job.

The solution came to me as I pondered some *Mysteries of Life*. A *Mystery of Life* is one of those things that happen all the time, but have no real logical reason *why* they happen. For example, why is it a small child must hear "please" and "thank you" about oh, ten thousand times, before it becomes part of their daily vocabulary—but they only need to hear a swear word ONCE and it becomes immediately cemented in their brain? I do not know. It is a *Mystery of Life*. Or, why does weight go *on* easier than it comes off? I don't know, it is a *Mystery of Life*. I first heard this idea when I listened to the tape by Jim Rohn, creator of the tape series, *The Art of Exceptional Living* (see chapter 9). He claims he used to lose sleep trying to figure these things out. Now that he has this *Mystery of Life* category, he claims he "sleeps like a baby!"

In school, students will work hard for five points extra credit, but ignore a paper that is worth forty points. Why is this? I do not know. It is a *Mystery of Life*. What I *did* find, though, was once I got beyond trying to figure out *why* these things are, I was able to accept them and I began using them to *my* advantage. You can too. Here's how.

I began to use what I call the "Quality Bonus" for papers done in class.

Students are able to earn up to five points extra credit if they satisfy a given list of quality standards. For example, I might require that they have a "complete heading, complete title, copy the question in ink and write the answer in pencil, skip a line between questions, the paper needs to be neat, complete and in the turn-in box by the end of class." (See *figure 3-3* at the end of this chapter for a sample overhead.) Students *slave* during class time. This works great because class time is used well (no closing the book and saying "I'll do it tonight for homework." Like THAT will really happen!). I know the paper has not been copied, because the work is happening right before my eyes. Since students are doing the work in class (and it's OK with their peers because of the extra credit), I can be there to offer help—or better yet, facilitate students helping students.

With this method most students' papers are done during the class period, except for the absent people. We all know it is much easier to grade a set of papers than to grade one'sy two'sy late papers. Now, I do not grade the papers for accuracy, I grade them for the quality bonus. You see, it's more work for a student to make up answers than to just do them correctly, so I know if the paper was completed, chances are it is mostly correct. So I quickly glance through to make sure the paper is complete, and write the plus five for the "Quality Bonus" at the top of the paper. Make it a rule of thumb that you will not spend more total time on a class set of papers than the students spent creating the paper. After all WE ALREADY KNOW THIS STUFF!

The students need to interact with the material three or four times if we want new material to have a chance of "sticking." The next class period, students pick up their papers before class starts, at the desk or counter by the door where the Early Work is. We correct the paper together in class. They put their score, plus the bonus, at the top of the paper, turn it in to the box, and I put it in the grade book. Now it's true that I handle the paper twice, but only for a few seconds each time. I usually spend about five minutes *total time* for each class! Part of the reason I can do this so quickly is that the papers come in at the "Quality Standard." (See figure 3-4 and 3-5 at the end of this chapter for a student sample done to the "Quality Standard".)

Another great part about the "Quality Standard" is the lack of rebellion against the request. If I were to say "I want the paper to look like this," I would receive all kinds of, "Well, I thought this was good enough." However, the "Quality Standard" provides an impersonal standard that they may choose to meet or not, but if they don't, "It's gonna cost ya!" Students may rebel against what the *teacher* wants, but they rarely rebel against the "Quality Standard." There is even more support for WIIFM in stereo in the next part. Read on.

How to increase student desire to complete work and do make-up work promptly

Our young adults do not see very far into the future. One of the frequently asked questions goes something like, "Why do we have to do this? How is this going to benefit *me?"* Responding how it will be good for them in their adult life does not seem to motivate them!

I'm going to share with you what works for me, but first you have to promise to read this whole passage! I'm going to ask you to think deviantly (educationally speaking). Consider this suggestion seriously, then do what you think is best—of course.

Ready? Here we go! Change the focus of your tests. After all, where does the learning take place? That's right, in the *daily* work. If we can think of a way to get students to do their daily work with a concern for accuracy, the learning will increase. So, rather than using tests to check on the learning, use the test as a reward for the daily work. Believe me, WIIFM will be playing loudly in stereo if you do this.

All reward-for-daily-work tests are matching and fill in the blank. The questions are taken *directly* from the daily work. Students are allowed to use anything *in their handwriting* as a reference during the test. Tests are timed, one minute for each question. So, a twenty question test will be allowed twenty minutes. (My special education students have the option of finishing before or after school, or with their special education teacher.)

By amending your tests in this way, it is clear to students that there is a reason *immediately important to them* for why the work should be completed, and completed correctly, before test day. For the first time ever, I actually have students correcting their papers and putting the correct answer in, if they had it wrong. The tests are easy to correct, so I can quickly give feedback. This quick feedback is valuable for the continued on-time completion of papers. So now if a student says, "Man, I flunked Mrs. LaBelle's test." There is no compassion from the peers.

Do you know how nice it is to hear the other students say, "All you have to do is the daily work. What did you do, nothing?" The unsuccessful student then says something like, "Hey, I had to work forty hours last week and I didn't sleep well, so I couldn't concentrate on school." Now we are getting someplace. You see, as long as the mean old teacher can be blamed, the student is angry at the teacher and feels helpless. Now the student knows s/he is *responsible* and therefore s/he can be in *control of change*. The next test's outcome depends on the *student's* choices, not the mean old teacher.

Responsibility Moving-overmanship is a sweet thing!

One last thing about tests. I took a class on how to write a test. In order to write a good test, one that *really* tests what we think we are testing is very hard and time consuming. Sometimes we are not testing what we think we are. At least, with the reward-for-daily-work test, I know what I am testing. "Did you do your daily work, did you correct it correctly, and can you re-access the information?" These are school-to-work skills.

Test points comprise half the student's grade in my class. In addition to the reward-for-daily-work tests, I assign "test points" for reports, speeches and the occasional essay questions. If you really want to give an essay test, make it a separate test from the reward-for-daily-work test. You see, I'm not saying, "Make all your test points a reward-for-daily-work," but do include this type of test and I guarantee you will see an improvement in the *quality* of daily work and the quantity of daily work completed on a timely basis. Students become concerned because it will immediately affect their grade. And that's about how far ahead some of our young adults can see—IMMEDIATELY!

Figure 3-1

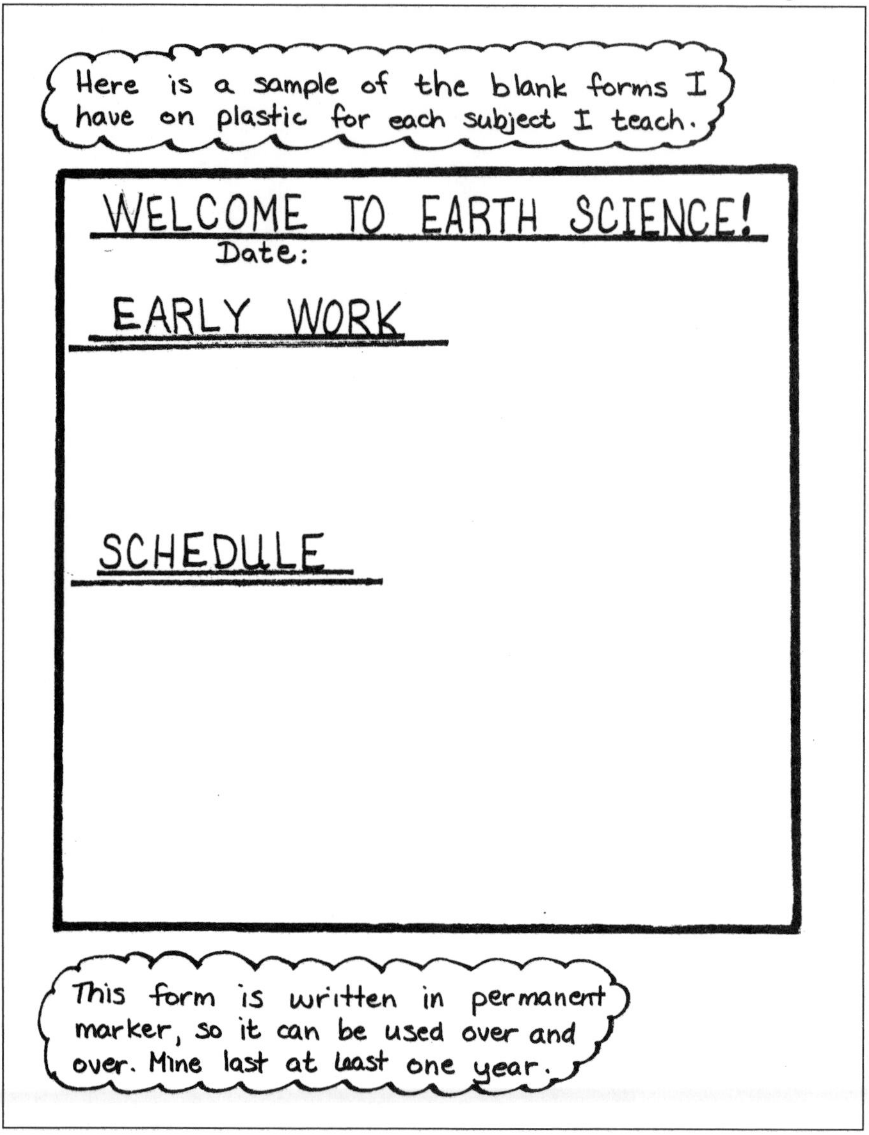

Here is a sample of the blank forms I have on plastic for each subject I teach.

WELCOME TO EARTH SCIENCE!

Date:

EARLY WORK

SCHEDULE

This form is written in permanent marker, so it can be used over and over. Mine last at least one year.

Figure 3-2

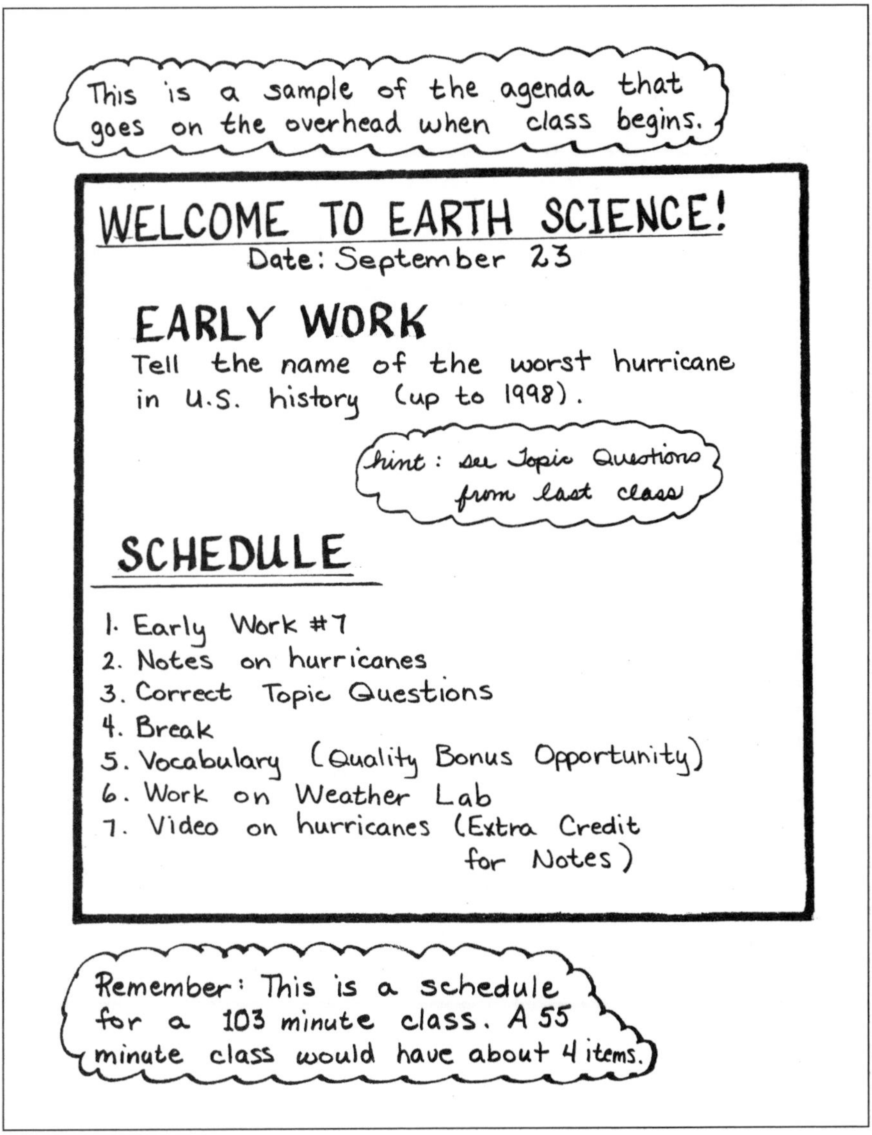

This is a sample of the agenda that goes on the overhead when class begins.

WELCOME TO EARTH SCIENCE!

Date: September 23

EARLY WORK

Tell the name of the worst hurricane in U.S. history (up to 1998).

hint: see Topic Questions from last class

SCHEDULE

1. Early Work #7
2. Notes on hurricanes
3. Correct Topic Questions
4. Break
5. Vocabulary (Quality Bonus Opportunity)
6. Work on Weather Lab
7. Video on hurricanes (Extra Credit for Notes)

Remember: This is a schedule for a 103 minute class. A 55 minute class would have about 4 items.

Figure 3-3

Sample of overhead plastic used to model standard for Quality Bonus

Begin 1:00
Finish 1:30
Break 1:30-1:35

First + Last Name
Earth Science P.3
Date

Topic Questions: pg 347
#1 b,c,d #3b #5a #6 b,c

Quality Bonus

complete heading
complete title
neat and complete
question in ink
answer in pencil
skip a line
in box by end of class

I put this on the overhead EVERY TIME we do a Quality Bonus activity

Figure 3-4

Score to go into grade book → +16/14

Quality Bonus → +5

Topic Questions pg 347
#1 b,c,d #3b #5a #6b

First & Last Name
Earth Science P.2
Date

#1 b): What is the general circulation pattern of Ocean current north and south of the equator?
+2
North of the equator is clockwise and south of the equator is counterclockwise.

+2 c): Within an ocean basin, where are warm currents generally found?

+1 The warm currents are on the west side of the ocean basin toward from equator

d): Within an ocean basin, where are cool currents generally found?

The cool currents are on the east side of the ocean basin, away from equator

#3 b): How does the Gulf Stream affect climates?
+2
carries warm water to Iceland & the British Isles, they now have warmer climates.

#5 a): Within an ocean basin, in what direction do cold currents flow?
+1

Toward the equator on the east side of ocean basins. clockwise

Sample of Quality Bonus paper

#6b c were on back

Figure 3-5

#6 b): Describe the location and origin of the Equatorial Countercurrents.

+2

The Equatorial countercurrent are surface currents that flow eastward between the westward moving North & South Equatorial. They developed in the Pacific Ocean, Atlantic and Indian Oceans.

c): Locate and describe the Cromwell Currents.

+2

They flow eastward underneath the westward flowing South Equatorial currents. Its a subsurface of the Pacific but occurs in the Atlantic and Indian Ocean. Its about 30 meters below surface: 210 meters thick and 400 kilo wide. Its average rate of speed is 1.5 meters per second.

CHAPTER 4

Sleep Deprivation and Competency

Here are a few more concepts I try to cover in the first few days. One is the concept of sleep deprivation. Sleep deprivation is such a national problem even Oprah devoted a whole show to it. In America, we have so much to fill our days. Back when computers were first becoming popular, (there I go, showing my age again!) we were assured the computer would make our lives simpler. Wellll, didn't work out that way! I once read that the average American receives more information in *one day* than the pioneers got in *one year.* Add to that the use of electronic devices and cell phones and it gets a little crazy. What happened to "down time?" In order to get everything done, we only have one place to get the time. We frequently rob from sleep time.

The increase in accidents where cars go off the road, with no evidence of braking, points to an increase in people falling asleep at the wheel. Sadly, we lost a fine young man from our high school due to sleep deprivation. He was working two jobs to earn money for college. On his way home from the night job, he fell asleep at the wheel and his car crossed the center line into a large truck.

Students need to know the symptoms of sleep deprivation. They need to know it is slow to come on and slow to go away—WE NEED TO KNOW IT TOO. I have included some pages, suitable for copying, if you would like to make plastic overlays for a short presentation to your class. (See *figure 4-1* at the end of this chapter). Please do cover this topic. It is important for us all to know that maybe everyone else is not irritating, maybe we are just sleep deprived and irritable! I have not found that awareness reduces the number of people who are robbing sleep time. However, it does make a difference in how students and teachers react to it.

When presenting this overhead, be sure to cover up the data and uncover one part at a time. This keeps students focused on *just* what you are talking about.

One of the "tests" for sleep deprivation is, "Can you fall asleep in 10 minutes or less in the middle of the day?" This question usually brings comments like, "Dude, I've got it!" like it's a disease. I guess in a way it *is* an American epidemic.

If we are all aware of the signs of sleep deprivation, at least we will realize we are seeing the world through tired eyes, and not how the world may really be. We also can take comfort in the fact that it may not always have to be this way. There is a "cure."

I have found that students are less reluctant to write reminders to themselves like, "test—earth science—Wednesday on chapter 12," if they feel it is because of sleep deprivation, rather than thinking it is because we think they are stupid.

Levels of Competency

Another concept for the first week of school, or first week of implementing *Teaching Smarter*, is the clear definition and differentiation between "helping" and "enabling." In my classes I use some terms I picked up at one of the conferences I attended. They are, "unconscious incompetent, conscious incompetent, unconscious competent and conscious competent." Whenever we can use new words for learners, it helps in presenting new ideas. It is hard for any learner, at any age, to attach *new* meanings to *old* words.

I have included a sheet for copying on *figure 4-2* at the end of this chapter. This is what I say when presenting this plastic sheet on the overhead (Remember, uncover one item at a time):

> UNCONSCIOUS INCOMPETENT—This is the person who does not know that they do not know. We all know someone who is an unconscious incompetent. Cliff Clavin on the series "Cheers" was an unconscious incompetent. He was always shooting his mouth off about every subject ever brought up—frequently without any real knowledge. For young people especially, if one tries to correct the unconscious incompetent, they simply TALK LOUDER OVER YOUR VOICE. This person does not listen to or seek help from others—after all they already know all the answers!
>
> CONSCIOUS INCOMPETENT—This is the person who knows they do not know. This person wants to know and will research or listen to others to find out the answer. It is OK to be a conscious incompetent. All lifelong learners are frequently conscious incompetents. However, if we are looking for help, the unconscious competent cannot really help us. We need to find a conscious competent who will guide us through the steps to knowledge.
>
> UNCONSCIOUS COMPETENT—This is someone who does not know HOW they came to know. If someone asks for help on an assignment, this person *cannot* explain it so the other person can learn. If I ask an unconscious competent to help me, they will usually try, but soon give up in exasperation. Usually the unconscious competent will end up saying, "Here, just copy my paper." This may get me my points, but come test time I am no smarter. Also, I am left with the feeling that I am not smart enough to learn the concept. Not a good feeling!

CONSCIOUS COMPETENT—This is someone who knows HOW they came to know. Hopefully, most of our teachers are conscious competents. A conscious competent is the person who can help me get smarter and do better on my next test. Not only that, conscious competents remember how hard it was to first learn the concept. They help me go away smarter and feeling good about myself.

By explaining the "stages of knowledge" we can *really help* students to understand that "telling" a friend the answer is *not* "helping." I sometimes tell this story, "No matter how much one describes how to swim, a person does not learn how to swim unless they get wet! Likewise, if I tell someone an answer, I have not allowed my friend to learn how to find the answer. They have not gotten 'wet.' That means the next time this person is stuck, they will have to seek me out for help *again*. Our goal is to help our friends get *smarter* and *more independent!*" This explanation precludes any "cheating" rules we might need to go over and we get a lot more "buy in."

Students respond so much better to explanations designed to help them honor their friends' intelligence. For example, saying something like, "look on page 59, paragraph two" is so much better than assuming someone is stupid, so "I better just tell them the answer." Not only that, but the next time the friend needs help, they will have learned how to find the answer, so we have helped them in more ways than just finding that one answer. Share with students that they can help their classmates get smarter by not enabling them. After a few times, it is so great to look out on my classroom and see students acting as mentors to their friends, and not just "cheating" to the right answer!

Teachers too. We need to think about the difference between helping and enabling. For example, a student comes into a classroom without pen or pencil. The first person the student comes to is the teacher for a bail-out. DON'T DO IT! I share this story with students, "If I was a mechanic, and I took my tools home to work on my car one weekend, then forgot to bring my tools back on Monday, what would I do? Would I go up to my boss and ask to borrow his or her tools? Not if I want to keep my job very long! I would go to my coworkers to bail me out. The LAST person I want to expose my forgetfulness to is my manager! The same is true in this classroom. If you ask me for a pencil, pen, paper or book, I will facilitate your borrowing from someone in class—but then, you could do that for yourself. If you do it for yourself, be sure to do it in a way that the 'manager' does not notice. After all, the purpose here is for the manager to be unaware you forgot your 'tools' and came to 'work' unprepared."

Maybe your students are much more reliable than most of mine, but I used to find that many of my loaned pens or pencils were not returned without a reminder from me, and I was frequently too busy to remember who borrowed what—until after class! Student and loaned working tool were long gone by then! The loaning *students* are much more likely to remember who borrowed what. Also, the same person who has no problem borrowing something from me every day, does not like borrowing from classmates. Classmates give the borrower some immediate negative "feedback" after a couple of times! Peers are not about to support a habit of being unprepared.

There is a simple test for whether we are enabling or helping. If the student behavior continues to need *us* for success, it is enabling. Punishment does not seem to extinguish enabling-seeking behavior (at least not very quickly). However, peer disapproval does. Remember, peers can say things to each other that I may think—but I'm too professional to say out loud. If the student behavior is independent after a few times, we are *helping* the student to self dependency.

HELPING QUICKLY REDUCES A TEACHER'S INVOLVEMENT, ENABLING REQUIRES ONGOING TEACHER ENERGY.

Figure 4-1

Sleep Deprivation

A short time solution to a long time problem

SLEEP DEPRIVATION

- Less than enough sleep for two weeks or more
- Fall asleep in 10 minutes or less in the middle of the day
- Young adults need 8 to 10 hours of sleep per night (more if they are in a sport or are working out)
- One cannot "make up" the lost sleep in a weekend

SYMPTOMS:

1. impatient
2. irritable
3. less logical
4. memory dysfunction

Figure 4-2

Stages of Knowledge

1. You do not know that you do not know (Unconscious Incompetent)
2. You know that you do not know (Conscious Incompetent)
3. You do not know how you know (Unconscious Competent)
4. You know how you know (Conscious Competent)

CHAPTER 5

Responsibility moving-overmanship, make-up work, increasing student grade awareness & processing absent student papers

Recognize this scene? A student has been absent for one or more class periods. During class, usually while I'm busy, the student comes up to me and asks for work missed. I reply that I am busy and will tell them later. Then I get even busier. The student does not remind me. The next thing I know the class is over and the student has left the classroom.

Picture this, dinner that night at the student's home, (Question) "Suzie, did you get the work you missed in Mrs. LaBelle's class?" (Answer) "I tried, but she didn't tell me." Whose fault is it that Suzy did not get her homework? That's right, mine. This is a prime spot for student responsibility moving-overmanship. Here's how I do it.

It is a given that most students are not going to give up "their time" before or after class to get homework. They prefer to use class time for that. So, how could I make it *their* responsibility to get work missed with a minimal interaction with me? I tried telling them to ask two friends before me. That worked marginally well—but the final responsibility was still mine. What I now do is this, I take a piece of butcher paper about 12 inches wide and about 3 feet long. This paper is taped vertically on a cupboard door or somewhere students can easily get to it. At the top of the butcher paper is the name of the class written in large felt tip pen. Below the class name I write the schedule, just as it appeared on the overhead for the day. Each day's entry is written in a different color felt tip pen, so it is easy to see where one day's schedule ends and the next day's schedule begins. To the right of the schedule list I put the day and date. I include any important messages, like "TEST Tuesday."

Now it is the *student's* responsibility to go to the butcher paper and write down what was missed during an absence. If students have a question about what was missed, I do not help them until I see that they have written down the schedule from the butcher paper. Some of your students will not like this method. I even had one student tell me that writing down what was missed during an absence was *my* job not his!

The way I first reinforce using the butcher paper is to remind, remind, remind for the first two weeks. Then when a student comes up to me and says, "What did I miss last time?" I just smile (be sure to smile nicely, this is a "friendly" reminder) and point to the butcher paper. The first few times I may get a confused look, then they go, "Oh yeh, I forgot."

This method is particularly helpful to special education aides. They do not need to have me in the classroom in order to see what students are responsible for. If a student claims they did not know an assignment was due, all one has to do is "check the butcher paper." I tell students, "If I forget to write it on the butcher paper, you will be excused from the assignment." So *you know,* I'm very good about keeping the butcher paper up to date! Usually, there are a few minutes during class when I can fill in the butcher paper for that day's schedule. If not, it only takes one or two minutes at the end of the day. If I forget, and I change classrooms, I just save the plastic schedule sheet (see, that's why I recommended several copies of the schedule form). Then I do the butcher paper fill-in the next class day.

Some of my workshop participants have made xerox copies of the schedule and put it in a notebook for students to reference. I have found that this option carries the risk of papers being removed from the three ring binder. It seems that some of the same students who are frequently absent are also too lazy to copy the work missed, so they take the paper out to copy and return (I'm being nice here aren't I?). Darndest thing, they forget to return the original paper! Now I have a "hole" in my record of activities done each day. However, the notebook DID come in very handy for one of my workshop participants. During a particularly difficult parent conference, where the parent was claiming that Johnny never knew about assignments, the teacher used the schedule notebook in an unexpectedly beneficial way. She simply showed the parent the schedule copy notebook, and explained the class start routine. The parent then focused the frustration on the student—where I believe it belonged in the first place! Responsibility moving-overmanship can be a wonderful thing!

Let's talk about what to do about the papers returned when a student is absent. Remember those Rubbermaid tubs we talked about before? I also use them to put the absent peoples' papers in. When I put papers on the table or counter by the door for student pick up before class, I have no idea who will be absent. However, during the Early Work time, I take attendance, then I go back by the door and pick up the absent peoples' papers. Now, if I keep those papers to return next time, whose responsibility is it to make sure the students get the papers? That's right, it's mine. However, since I have become a believer in responsibility moving-overmanship, I no longer do that. Right below the butcher paper schedule, or very near it, I put a colored Rubbermaid tub. I use a different color for each subject, and never the same color as the turn-in box. We work with very visual kids (a product of the T.V. age?). Color can really be our friend! In the Rubbermaid tub close to the butcher paper schedule, I put all papers not collected by students before class started. Now, whose responsibility is it to get the absent person's papers? Yes, it is the *students'* responsibility. I even put extra copies of worksheets in the tub. That way students can pick up papers, check the butcher paper and get whatever worksheet they may be missing. These days, I rarely even have to interact with a student who has been absent. They know what to do, and I have structured for their independent success. Station WIIFM again is playing in stereo. The student does not have to wait on me, and I do not have to wait on the student!

How to have students aware of their grade at any time, and how to make them aware of all assignments that make up their grade

The computer is a wonderful thing, and I know many of us use them for figuring grades. Please consider this. The computer can make our lives easier, but are we also using the computer combined with responsibility moving-overmanship? I have seen many teachers move into the computer age, but maintain the same level of teacher responsibility. If we are to prepare students for the world of work, or the world of college, or the world of life beyond school, we need to help them take responsibility. Sometimes, with the best of intentions for helping students, we are enabling them into total dependence on us. That's not good for them, and it's not good for us.

With that philosophy in mind, think about this. If all the grades are in the computer, and any time a student wants to know their grade, you have to access the program and give them a print out, who is responsible? If Mom or Dad says "Oglethorp, did you find out your grade in Mrs. LaBelle's class today?" Is Oglethorp in a position to say, "I asked Mrs. LaBelle, and she didn't give it to me." If the answer is yes, there is a better way. You guessed it, responsibility moving-overmanship.

In my class students are given a form I call the Personal Grade Book (or PGB). This is just a piece of brightly colored paper with lines on it. In my classes 50% of a student's grade is their daily work (another encouragement to do the daily work—and a place where they have a lot of control over their grade), and 50% of the grade is test grades (this is made up of daily-work-reward tests, essay tests, presentations or anything else I want to give "test importance" to). I have included a sample of a blank PGB (Personal Grade Book) and a filled in PGB on figures 5-1 and 5-2 at the end of this chapter.

Each time a student's paper is returned or a test grade is shared, I put a plastic sheet on the overhead showing my copy of what their PGB should look like (model, model, model). I tell them, "These are the scores I have in my grade book at this time. If someone were to ask what your grade is at this time, these are the scores I would base my answer on." With this method, no student has a right to act surprised at their grade. Even students who refuse to fill out their own PGB, have seen what they are responsible for on the overhead. If a student wants to compare their numbers with mine, they must first show me a completed PGB form. I keep extra blanks available, so if they "lost" or "left the PGB at home" they can recopy it from a friend, or from my plastic. Be *very* consistent here. Your "responsibility resistant" student will try many times to get out of accountability. I have found that some students are very comfortable with having the *teacher* responsible, and it takes some "cornering" and "encouragement" to get them to buy into self dependence. Keep in mind, some of our young friends are natural *experts* at not taking responsibility, but WE ARE OLDER AND SMARTER!

The PGB is also very handy when a parent wants to support me, but has no idea what assignments the student has missed. In the past I would sometimes feel *I* was putting more effort into certain student's work than they were! With the PGB, the student has to bring me a copy of the completed PGB. I will then highlight the assignments that are missing. If the assignment involves pages in the book, the student can go to the butcher paper to get the pages. Some students are very resistant, but eventually they realize, "I might as well do this. If I don't, Mrs. LaBelle will make me do even more work to make it up." Parents have been very supportive of this method, and I don't even have to be involved for more than about one minute, just enough time to highlight. By highlighting, I am not saying the student did not *do* the work, I am saying the work was not *turned in.* The highlighting also is a nice way for parents to see how much work the student *has* done, rather than just focusing on what has not been done!

I don't know how your particular school district works, but in mine we have Progress Reports every mid-quarter, we have quarter grades, and we have the permanent semester grades. At each of these reporting periods, I share what "my grade book says your grade is." The words I use are carefully chosen. I do not say, "Here's what I say your grade is." That way is too personal, and invites conflict. It's much harder to get mad at a grade book than it is to get mad at a teacher. I also share with my students that I try to be perfect in my grade book, but with 150 students, chances are there will be at least one mistake. By sharing what the grade book says the current score is, it puts the responsibility on the student (sound familiar?) to tell me if there is a mistake. I call it their chance for a final "Okey, Dokey." THEY approve and agree with the scores I report, or THEY take the responsibility (there's that word again!) to help correct it. After all, I want to be 100% correct in my record keeping—but I need their help.

Many of our students have been "parentally maintained" (i.e. Parents have provided food, water, clothing, and other basic needs and wants.) but perhaps not "parentally socialized" (ie. Young people have not been taught to use please and thank you or how to politely approach someone with whom they disagree.). We may not like it, but the job is sometimes ours to teach students how to approach a situation where there may be a problem. We have to teach the students from where they ARE, not from where they SHOULD BE. I actually model for the students how to approach me if they feel there has been an error in the grade book. I say, "Look, basically you are trying to motivate me to change something to your favor. I am a person. I am not motivated by someone coming up to me and saying, 'This is wrong' while slapping the paper down with a ticked off look on their face." I actually make the face and slap the paper down. The students usually laugh. After all, none of THEM would ever act like that! Then I show them how to approach me and suggest to them that they say something like, "My PGB does not have the same total as yours. Could we compare numbers and see where the difference happens?" Then I smile and say, "How could anyone not want to help a polite person like that?" They all agree. It's amazing, those are the EXACT words I get back to me when there is a problem. But that's OK, it's polite!

I encourage students to keep their papers, not only for the tests, but also if my grade book does not show a paper's score, and the student is sure it was done, the student simply shows me the paper. There is no way I will remember *a* paper on *a* day from *a* student. I make sure to share this fact with students early in the course. "Keep your papers until you are SURE you will not need them." I never collect notebooks, because different learning styles have different ways of accessing information. However, students quickly see the benefit of keeping papers where they can access them. This is a school-to-life skill. If one cannot find papers in the home or at the office, they are in a world of hurt. With all the paperwork that comes to our work and our home, there is no way we can remember it all. We are doing our students a great favor if they learn how to handle paperwork in a way that makes sense to them.

There you have it. By using these techniques you will have students who are responsible for finding out what they missed during an absence, students who know where to get papers returned during their absence, students who know what their grade is at any time, students who know how to file and retrieve papers, and even students who know how to approach a disagreement politely!

CAN'T YOU JUST FEEL YOUR CLASSROOM LIFE GETTING EASIER?

Figure 5-1

Each student has a copy of this form, printed on a bright colored paper.

PERSONAL GRADE BOOK (PGB)

Name ______________________ Code Number ______________

Class ______________________ Period ______________

Seatwork		Tests	

Remember, this form not only keeps track of grades. It also keeps students aware of papers due and can be a great parent-communication tool.

Figure 5-2

This is a sample of what the teacher's overhead plastic might Look like. Students' copies have their scores filled in.

PERSONAL GRADE BOOK (PGB)

Name *Sample* Code Number 15

Class *Earth Science* Period 2

Seatwork (½ of Grade)		Tests (½ of grade)	
Early Work Pkt	/50	Glaciers	/32
Recent Glaciers Chart	/20	Earth History	/30
Vocab. on Glaciers	/44	Prog. Rpt. Total	/62
Iceberg Chart	/20	Prog. Rpt. %	
Era Chart	/40		
Chart of Life	/50		
Vocab. on Earth History	/30		
Progress Report Total	/254		
Progress Report %			

We update the PGB about once a week. It is important to update the PGB frequently.

CHAPTER 6

Using time to your benefit for class dismissal and for in-class work time

There is a sad sight I sometimes see when walking by a classroom door. I see students crowded by the door, frequently with one or two yelling out, "Can we go now?" It's not good for the teacher, or the students. (They seem to begin "stacking the door" earlier and earlier as they test the teacher's tolerance—thus losing valuable class time.) Nor is it good for our image should we have visitors in the building, which seems to be happening more and more.

Beginning with the first day, it is important students realize that the bell, if there is one, is the *teacher's* signal that class is over. Then the teacher, not the bell, will dismiss the students. Make sure students know *they* are in control of how quickly dismissal will happen, even though it is the *teacher* who dismisses the students. Establish your "Quality Standard for Dismissal." All students are seated at their assigned seat and quiet. (Yes, you need to be that specific.) I have had students try standing *by* their seat, *near* their seat, *kneeling* on their seat. Expect to be tested. Be firm. Simply say, "I'm ready to dismiss, but I still see someone not seated at their assigned seat." Let the peers "encourage" the suboptimizer to cooperate. Always position yourself as the kind teacher who is ready and willing to dismiss the class, as soon as EVERYONE has met the quality standard. Once again, you use the "quality standard" rather than saying this is what *I* want. Using the word "I" sets yourself up for adolescent rebellion. If a particular student wants attention by holding up the class, I simply say, "Student's Name, since *you* had a particularly tough time meeting the quality standard, it's only fair that you be the last student to leave the classroom today." When dismissed, there will be some students who walk out *very slowly.* This is the peers' way of negatively reinforcing the suboptimizer, after all it *is* pay back time! This way it is the *peers* negatively reinforcing the suboptimizer, and it is a much better way to extinguish the behavior. You have removed the "hero rebel" status, and replaced it with what the behavior really is, a cry for attention, at the expense of the peers.

In addition to everyone being in their assigned seats, the quality standard includes a neat classroom with no trash on the floor, books stacked neatly on counters, and tables and chairs in the original positions. One inventive teacher was having trouble with the last part of the quality standard because the classroom was left a mess from the previous class. This teacher applied the *Mystery of Life* extra credit option, and had students arguing over who got to clean-up the room for five extra credit points!

Of course, the quality standard must be met before any "time" is served. (Remember that "How to get students' attention" piece from Chapter 3?)

It is important that we spend time on the basic rules in the first few weeks. Make sure the classroom management procedure is very clear. Practice the procedures. Use the all powerful "wait time" and do not proceed until you have 100% participation. Last, develop some type of signal phrase that is used EVERY DAY to dismiss the class. I use "See you next time." Believe me, the number of students cooperating and the learning opportunity for teaching how the classroom is managed will never be better than during the *honeymoon* of the first two weeks or so!

One tool I use is to write the quality standard expectations (notice I stay away from the word "rules") on the overhead as I say them. We are dealing with a visual population. They need to see it and hear it. Then the next day, guess what the Early Work question is? That's right, "What are the four quality standards that must be met before students are excused from this class?" The answer:

- everyone in their assigned seat and quiet,
- room neat,
- chairs and tables in the original positions,
- and books stacked neatly.

How to get students to use class time wisely

In addition to the "Quality Standard Bonus" described in chapter 3, there are a few more ways to help students use time more wisely in the classroom. I recommend that you do the "Close your eyes and guess one minute" activity described in Chapter 1 with your students sometime in the first few days. It will really help them realize that five minutes is a lot of time to get some things done. I've had students say, "Five minutes? That's not enough time to get ready to dismiss!" Soon they realize that two minutes is more than they need.

When papers are assigned to work on in class, I model the desired quality standard for the heading and title. Then I write the start time on the overhead. I also write an end time (Remember the sample on *figure 3-3?*). This helps students see that there is a finite expectation for finishing.

After about five minutes, I announce, "The *Teacher Prowl* is coming." They know this means I am going to walk around the classroom and just see how people have progressed. You and I both know the range is significant after only five minutes! If I pass by a group that is making minimal progress, I simply mention, "I will be back in about five minutes, be sure there has been significant progress, or I will have to ask you to not sit together at this time." Notice who has primary control here—the student. If I return after five minutes, and no significant progress has been made, then the "nice teacher" will have to move the students apart. There is no support for the misbehaving students from peers. After all, "She warned you and gave you a chance, and you blew it."

After I finish the *Prowl* I will announce, "Most of the class is well on their way to finishing number one" (or whatever the appropriate comment is). Once again, I remove myself from the authoritative position, to one of advisor. Who can argue with where most of the class is? Even if a student does argue, the rest of the class soon corrects the situation. Many times with this method, students will say things to suboptimizers that I would like to, but I am too professional to say out loud!

After a couple of *Prowls* I can tell if my guesstimate of how long the assignment should take is appropriate or not. Always guess short if you're not really sure. That way you can say, "You have all been working so hard and most of you are not quite done. Therefore I will extend the time by ten more minutes." If students do not feel that is enough, simply say, "If everyone is quietly working and needs more time I will be happy to give it." Once again you have structured the teacher into the hero roll. Isn't that nice?

Pace students. Many students who do not finish papers, are late starters. I have found some students wait so long to start, because thirty minutes seems sooo long. Then when they find there's not enough time to finish, they give up. By establishing a specific start time, implementing the *Prowl* and announcing, "The time is half over," no student can use THAT tired old excuse. Also, you have had several opportunities to watch the progress (or lack of it) through using the *Prowl*.

Currently, many schools are lengthening the time for each class. Much research has been done to show that ALL learners have the capacity to attend for an hour or more to things they are personally interested in. (To test this, just watch how well a five or six year old will stay focused playing video games!) However, and this goes for adults too, if one is *not* particularly interested in the topic, the optimum learning time is about twenty to thirty minutes. So, if we want to maximize student learning, we need to structure learning in blocks of about twenty minutes. One of the schools I worked in had class periods of 103 minutes (periods 1, 2, 3 one day and periods 4, 5, 6 the next day). Some teachers tried to just teach two 55 minute classes in one day. Not only does this not work for learning concepts, it results in lots of behavior problems because the students lost interest about an hour and a half ago! If we are going to teach in longer class periods, we need to remember that no matter what we do, some students will not have a burning interest in our subject. It is critical that we try to break the learning "bits" into about 20 to 30 minute chunks, then change. For example, rather than assigning one long task, analyze how it can be broken into several smaller tasks, preferably with different student groupings.

In longer periods I have also found it most advantageous to structure an "in-class break" into my schedule. My breaks are usually five minutes in length. There is a specific start time written on the overhead, and a specific end time written on the overhead. (Write it down, write it down, they *have* to see it.) I use the same old count down routine when the break comes to an end. It's amazing the difference a break can make. Students will watch the clock, and continue working (or "hold out") for the break. You see, we cannot stop students from taking a break during a long period. The reality is, we can either structure a break, or students will take one on their own. I guarantee that students will not all take their unstructured break together on their own! First the group in the back right corner will begin talking off task, then the other corner and then—well, you get the idea. If you're like most of us you've lived this scene before.

During the in-class five minute break is when students may use the restroom, or just chat quietly, or get up and walk around the room. Most of my students get out of their seats and quietly talk among themselves. This time is the appropriate opportunity for students to check grades, or talk privately with me. (This "opportunity" is handy to mention if we get the parent phone call that says Oglethorp never had time to find out his missing assignments—responsibility moving-overmanship.) It is also a nice time for me to gather my thoughts for the second half of the period, or to take a deep breath or two. Station WIIFM is playing in stereo again—darn, that's a great station!

CHAPTER 7

The Last Hints for Classroom Management

There are just a few more classroom management hints I want to share with you. Hints that have helped to manage my time in the classroom better.

1: Use colored paper. Color makes it so much easier to find items in a student's notebook. For example, all the Personal Grade Books are printed in bright yellow. When I want students to update their PGB, it is a simple matter to say, "Turn to your bright yellow Personal Grade Book." Even the most unorganized student can find the bright yellow paper in their notebook—if it is in there.

When I teach physics, I make each worksheet for the unit a different color. That way I can say, "Turn to worksheet number two, the one on blue paper." This simple technique can really reduce the paper shuffle, and it shows students a technique that I found very helpful in college. I still use it today at work and at home.

2: Use lots of points for work done. It is another *Mystery of Life* that students will work much harder for a 50 point paper than for a 5 point paper.

Even my physics students, who certainly have the math background, are more motivated by more points. Also, by using lots of points for daily work, you can afford to offer five point "Quality Standard Bonuses" without substantially tipping the point scale. Besides, 8 out of 10 is 80% and 800 out of 1000 is 80% and the grade is based on the percent, right?

Remember I divide the students' grades into two parts, 50% for test points and 50% for daily work. During one semester I may have 1,500 points for daily work and maybe only 400 points for tests. However, it does not matter because daily work is half the grade and test points are half the grade. The large number of daily points helps students realize *they* have lots of control over their grade. When the students feel in control, they work harder, more papers come in, class time is used more wisely and I can spend less time on make-up work (there's that WIIFM again).

3: Late work, ah yes, late work! I have tried to model a policy on late work that is tied to the work world. I do accept late work, because I want students to do the work and learn. However, "It's gonna cost ya" 10% per school day. I explain how in the world of work there are frequently penalty clauses in contracts for late delivery of goods because it results in additional time for other people in the system. The same is true in the classroom. A late paper requires more time on my part, which I am willing to do—but not for free! (Once again position yourself as the kind, but reasonably tough person.) I believe this is one more example of helping, but not enabling. One more thing about late work. I have a special box labeled "Late Work." All late papers are put in this box. It is my policy to grade all on-time papers quickly. Then, I will grade the late work in my *spare time.* I guarantee to have late work graded by the next grade report period, and students can check the "Late Box" at any time to make sure I haven't lost their paper. Students are OK with this rule. After all, *they* are the ones who turned in the paper late. Why should I drop everything to correct the paper right away? When I receive the paper, I put the received date at the top.

That way the 10% "charge" for late work is accurate. This technique of putting the date received at the top has saved me SO MUCH TIME. I no longer have to remember—I just look at the date I marked, so I don't have to grade the paper quickly "in case I might forget."

4: **Help, but do not enable.** I know, I already talked about this, but it is sooo important, I just wanted to say a few more words about it. Remember my statements about "maintenance parenting?" Maintenance parenting comes about because many families are working so hard at their jobs to make ends meet, that parenting has become the provision of basic physical needs and wants. These are important, of course. However, the provision of "things" is not all there is to parenting. There is the "proactive parenting" part. This is where the parent anticipates the social needs of the child. This includes such things as polite manners, how to approach a person with whom one disagrees (without aggression), how to be respectful (without losing self-esteem), or how to appreciate what others do for you.

I will never forget the time I took my 10 year old daughter and some of her friends to the roller skating rink. I pulled up to the front door, the kids piled out and my daughter was the *only* one to say, "Thanks for the ride." That was not too cool, but even worse, one of the girls said, "Why did you thank your MOM? You don't have to thank your Mom, it's her job to take you places." Can you believe it? This child thought it was her right to be served by her mom! What am I saying? Can this really be true? I know *you* know it's true because we see it in the classroom. We actually have students who feel it is our job to serve them like this little girl thought her mom "owed" her. (Lucky for my daughter, she replied, "If I expect my Mom to take me anywhere again, I better appreciate what she does today. She doesn't HAVE to take me anywhere. AND, you better say 'Thanks for the ride' or she will never take you anywhere either!" You know what? Later, when I dropped the kids off at their houses, EVERY KID thanked me for the ride! Two things I learned that day, my daughter does listen to me, and ALL KIDS CAN LEARN!)

"Helping" facilitates a child's growth and they become a more self-reliant and accepted part of our society. "Enabling" facilitates a child's dependence on someone else. Enabling will foster a belief that one's life is based on fate, that others are in control. Helping will bring the young person to the realization that s/he has lots of control over their life through the choices they make.

5: What about work missed during an absence? Help, but do not enable. The same goes for make-up work missed during an absence from class. Students have the day they come back to find out what they missed. (Remember the butcher paper and the Rubbermaid tub by the butcher paper list of schedules?) They have one day's "grace" and then the paper must be turned in on the third day, if they want full credit.

In addition, it is the student's responsibility to write the word "absent" at the top of the page. We need to point out to them that we are managers of 150 different students' papers. There is no way I will remember who was absent and who was late. So, without the word "absent" at the top of the paper, I have no choice but to assume the paper is late, and charge the 10% per day rule (Oh *what can* I do? See, there's that nice teacher again.)

Now, even if I *do* remember that the young person was absent, I still charge the 10% per day if they fail to write "absent" at the top. Then they usually come up very defensively and say, "But I was absent!" This is the "teachable moment." I ask them about the rule, then I say, "OK, everyone makes a mistake once in a while. However, next time I will have to charge you because now I have to go back to my grade book and change the grade, and that involves more work for me because of your error. You understand that, right?" (There's that nice teacher again!) See how that "teachable moment" is lost if I just take the paper back, change the grade and hand it back. Do you think the student is more or less likely to remember next time?

We are group managers, we are not the personal tutors of thirty students at once. There are a few young people who are not able to listen well to group instruction and need that personal touch. However, we must structure the individual instruction so it only happens ONCE, not over and over each time that student is absent and needs to turn in papers! In any situation like this, try to structure yourself as the nice teacher, who will let this happen just once, and make sure the student realizes the PERSONAL consequences if it happens again. Be sure they understand the *reason* for the rule.

6: Write page numbers on the overhead. Since we are dealing with a visual generation, it is a good idea to write as much on the overhead as possible. When I first started teaching, I bet I answered the "What page?" question 10 times every time we opened a book. After all, it's a great way to get the teacher's individual attention, without getting in trouble! Now I just write the page number on the overhead. When a student asks "What page?" I say nothing and just smile nicely (it's a friendly reminder) and point to the overhead. Do you see how answering, would be enabling? It doesn't take too many times before someone says, "What page?" and an exasperated classmate will say "Jeez, look at the overhead, how many times does it take?" (Something I would like to say, but I'm too professional to say out-loud).

7: Use the overhead to help when correcting papers. There are students in many of our classes who are what I call "singular processers." They only process one thing at a time. It really helps those kids to have things written on the overhead. That way they can process at their own speed and nobody has to know that they did not hear what "number five" was worth. I have included a sample of an overhead used during paper correction on *figure 7-1* at the end of this chapter.

8: Use a grid to show the students' test results. When I return tests, I make a chart on the overhead of the class scores, by letter grade. If I have more than one class of the same subject, I chart the results on one piece of plastic by period number. (See *figure 7-2* at the end of the chapter for a sample.) This really helps me, because I can see at a glance how the WHOLE group of students taking, say earth science, are doing on the tests. If you implement the reward-for-daily-work test system, your grades will typically cluster around the A-B range or the D-F range, with very few C grades. Either students do the work and do well on the test, or they don't do the work and do poorly on the test.

In the "old way" I would return tests and discuss them. Then the students who did poorly would gripe that the test was too hard, and all their buddies would agree. I would be on the defensive, and the students who *did* well would not speak up (you know, "The Code"). By charting the results with no names attached, students can easily see where their score fits into the totals for ALL students taking the test. By the way, if you ever do give a test that most students fail, it probably IS YOUR PROBLEM and a new test should be given after some review. Can you imagine how many "points" you would get with the students for doing something radical like that? However, by using the tools I have given you in previous chapters, it is highly unlikely that a new test will be needed. It has never happened for me in over ten years of using this technique. More likely what will happen is, a student says "Man, I flunked Mrs. LaBelle's test!" Rather than getting the typical positive pumps like, "Yeh, her tests are really hard." The student is more likely to hear "What did you do, nothing?" We talked about this in Chapter Three, but I wanted to bring it up again. It is so powerful to hear the peers not support the same old tired excuses of blame. It is also a method to put the student back in charge. The really important lesson here is that the student realizes the control he or she has over the grade that is earned.

9: You do not *give* grades. By the way, do not EVER buy into "What grade did *you give* me?" Whenever I hear this, and before I even begin to answer the grade question, I restate the question back as, "You mean 'What grade did I earn?' don't you?" I tell this story to the class early on in the year, "After a softball game, have you ever gone up to the score keeper and said, 'What score did you give my team?' Of course not! The same is true when computing your grade. My grade book is just a score-keeping of the grades YOU HAVE EARNED. So, if you want to check on your grade, it is much better to simply ask for the point total in my grade book. Please do not ask me what grade I *gave* you. I do not give grades. I provide *opportunities* for you to earn points so you can graduate and get on with your life."

10: Be sure you model quality. If we are going to reinforce a quality standard, we need to model what one looks like. The way we REALLY transmit the importance of something is by spending time on it. This certainly applies to the quality standards. We cannot afford to preach neatness, and then put charts on the wall that were done in two minutes! So make sure the charts you make are neatly lettered and hung straight. I know this seems obvious, but I only bring it up because I have seen ... well, you know. IF IT TRULY IS IMPORTANT WE SPEND TIME ON IT!

11: Create assignments that focus on just neatness. One of the ways I stress the importance of being neat, is to structure some papers where the grade is given on "neatness and completeness." Believe it or not, folks, some kids must have been absent when "neatness counts" was taught! I have students in the tenth grade who do not know how to hold a ruler to make a long straight line (the fingers are spread apart, so the ruler will not twist). I have had students in high school science classes who are not sure which side of the ruler is metric.

There are students who never heard of putting a dark-lined paper under a plain sheet of paper to make straight lines for lettering. I have students make a "line template" the first week of school. All it consists of is a sheet of notebook paper on which students use a ruler to darken in about twelve lines (pencil works best). This is an easy lesson in following directions. When done the first week of school, we can get some "interesting" feedback on the basic skills of some students. Tell students to put this paper in their notebook to be used for the rest of the semester from time to time. (I also quickly find out who can keep papers for future reference and who cannot.)

I know we are in the computer age, but many of the neatness rules still hold. For example, I was on a summer visit to one of our local businesses. The manager stressed the importance of neat penmanship on rejection tags. We *still* communicate in hand written form at times. Should these skills have been taught by someone else? I guess so, but OUR JOB IS TO TAKE KIDS FROM WHERE THEY *ARE,* AND NOT FROM WHERE THEY *SHOULD* BE. So, if it is important, we need to spend time on it. What I do is find some chart in the text that I'm pretty sure most kids have skipped over. Then I recreate it with the students, step by step, on the overhead. The students know that this is a "neatness and completeness" assignment, and it will earn them points, as well as have a question on the test. These papers are easy to grade, and it is a real eye-opener to see how hard this task is for many of my middle-to-lower achieving students. It is also great to see the pride they take in what may be one of the very few papers they have ever created that was more than just barely good enough to "make the teacher shut up and go away." I have included samples of "neatness and completeness" papers on *figures 7-3* and *7-4* at the end of this chapter. I intentionally chose papers completed by students who do not usually focus on neatness and completeness. They really struggle when neatness is the focus of the assignment, but if the quality standard is clearly explained, they can produce nice products that they can surprise *themselves* with!

12: Use a manila folder for each class to keep papers together for *just that class*. One of the best ways I've found to organize paperwork is to keep a file folder for each class in the classroom on my desk. Inside the folder, I staple a class seating chart and notes from parents, as well as other important papers for just that class. At one of my schools, we had blue days (periods 1,2,3) and gold days (periods 4, 5, 6). Therefore, I had blue folders for periods 1, 2, 3, and yellow folders for periods 4, 5, 6. That way, things may go crazy during the "doing" of the class period, but I at least have all the "period three" papers in the "period three" folder. I can sort the papers later if I need to. You see, color works for us too!

13: How to manage sets of papers. When working with class sets of papers, I have found it works best to "go vertical." By this I mean, take all the papers for a particular class, fold them in half the long way (like a hot dog bun) and put a rubber band around them. Make sure the writing is facing out so it is easy to see which set of papers is which. Then take a box and stand the rubber banded papers upright in the box. In this way I can have several class sets of papers ready to correct or return, and I can access them quickly. I have found this method works sooo much better than any "lay um flat" routine.

14: How to easily find your plastic forms. I purchase one brightly colored folder that has 2 pockets inside for holding papers (in Washington we call them Pee Chee folders). At the beginning of the year I make multiple plastic overheads of forms I use regularly in class. Some of the forms I have copies of are the Personal Grade Book, Early Work cover sheets, the Line Template, Skeleton Schedule forms for each class and graph paper forms.

It is sooo handy to have extra copies stored in a spot where I can quickly find them. No matter how messy my desktop gets, I can always put my hands on the red Pee Chee.

Figure 7-1

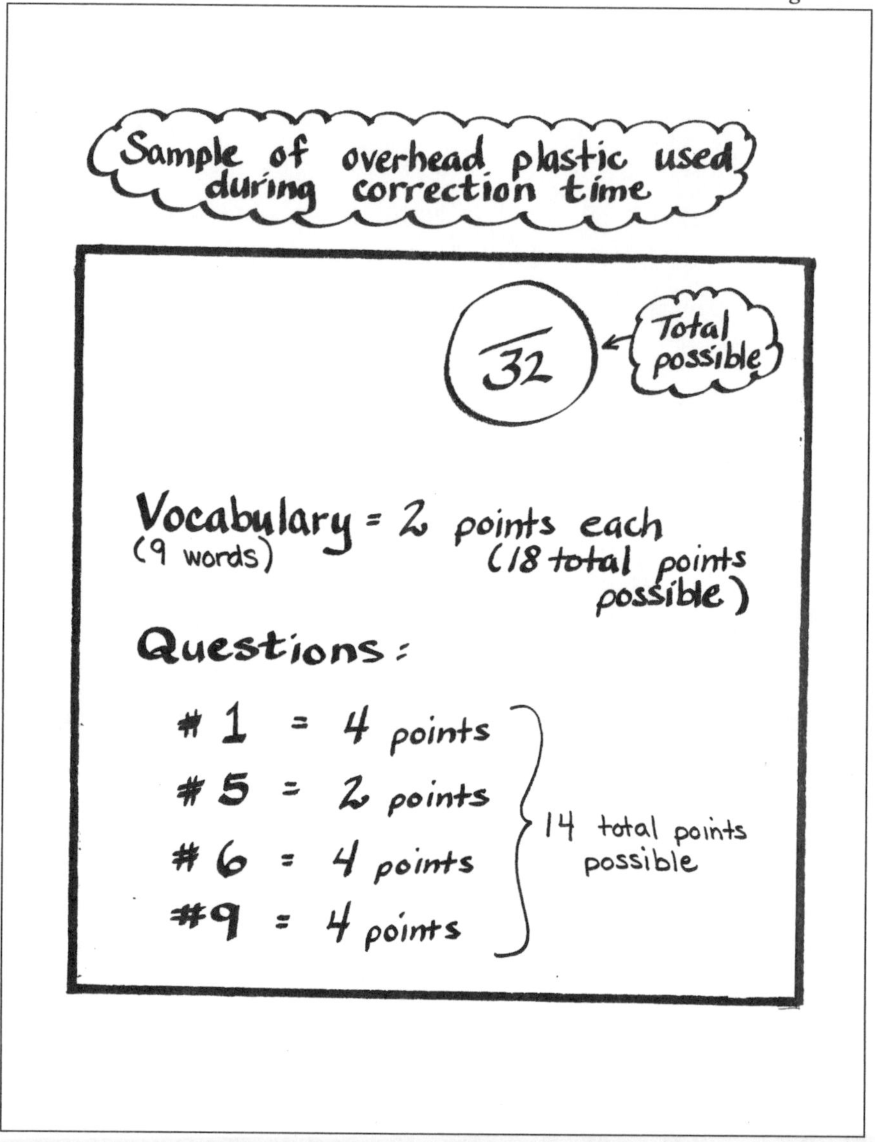

Sample of overhead plastic used during correction time

32 ← Total possible

Vocabulary = 2 points each
(9 words)
(18 total points possible)

Questions:

#1 = 4 points
#5 = 2 points
#6 = 4 points
#9 = 4 points

14 total points possible

Figure 7-2

Sample of overhead plastic used when tests are returned.

Test on Volcanoes (★ = perfect)			
Score	Per. 2	Per. 4	Total
40 - 36 A	7 ★	7	14 ★
35 - 32 B	3	7	10
31 - 28 C	2	4	6
27 - 24 D	3	1	4
23 - 0 (not passing)	1	4	5
Zero (did not take)	2	3	5

These classes had 8-12 special education students in each class.

Figure 7-3

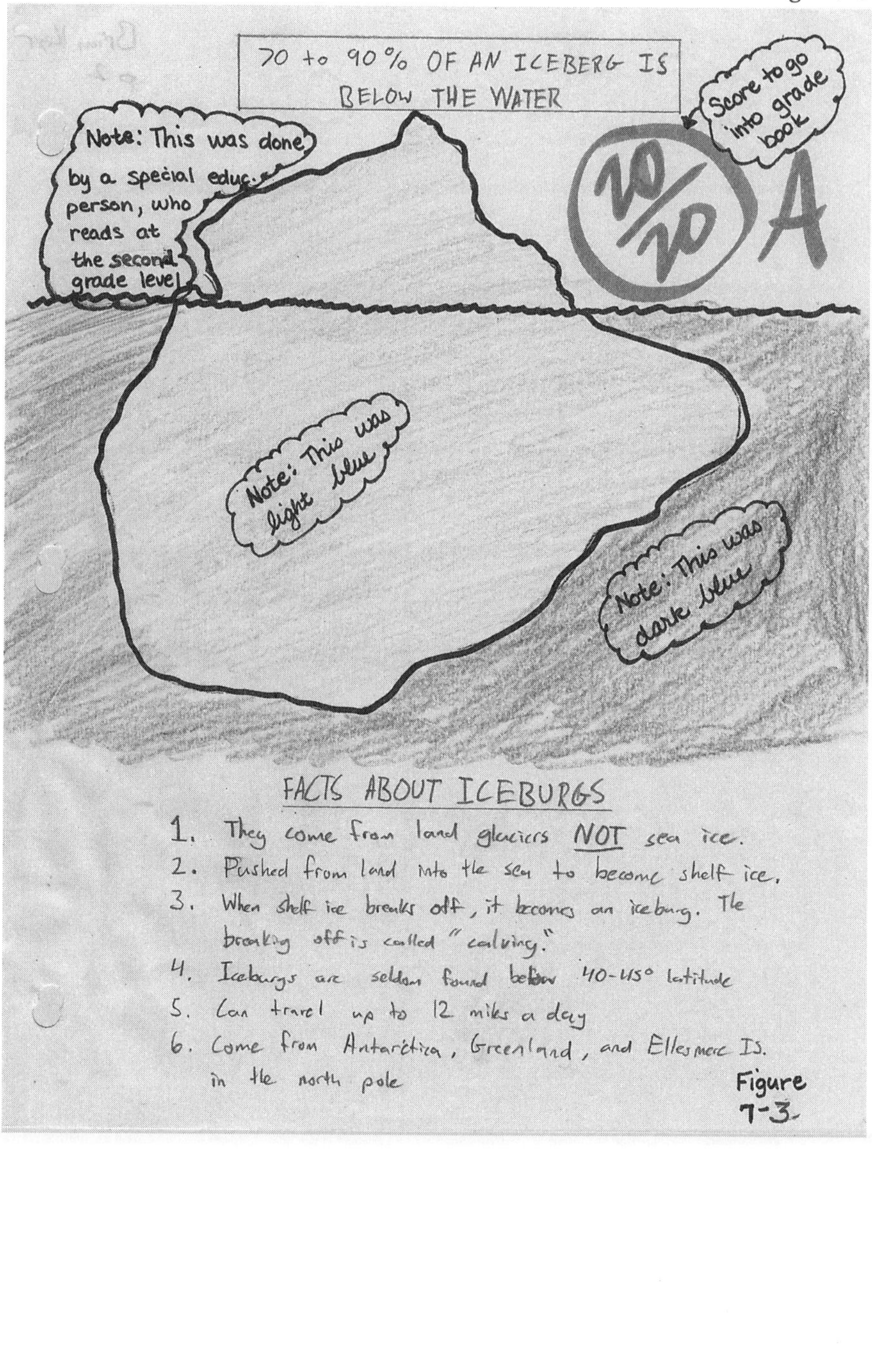

70 to 90% OF AN ICEBERG IS BELOW THE WATER

Note: This was done by a special educ. person, who reads at the second grade level

Score to go into grade book

20/20 A

Note: This was light blue

Note: This was dark blue

FACTS ABOUT ICEBURGS

1. They come from land glaciers NOT sea ice.
2. Pushed from land into the sea to become shelf ice.
3. When shelf ice breaks off, it becomes an iceburg. The breaking off is called "calving."
4. Iceburgs are seldom found below 40-45° latitude
5. Can travel up to 12 miles a day
6. Come from Antarctica, Greenland, and Ellesmere Is. in the north pole

Figure 7-3

Figure 7-4

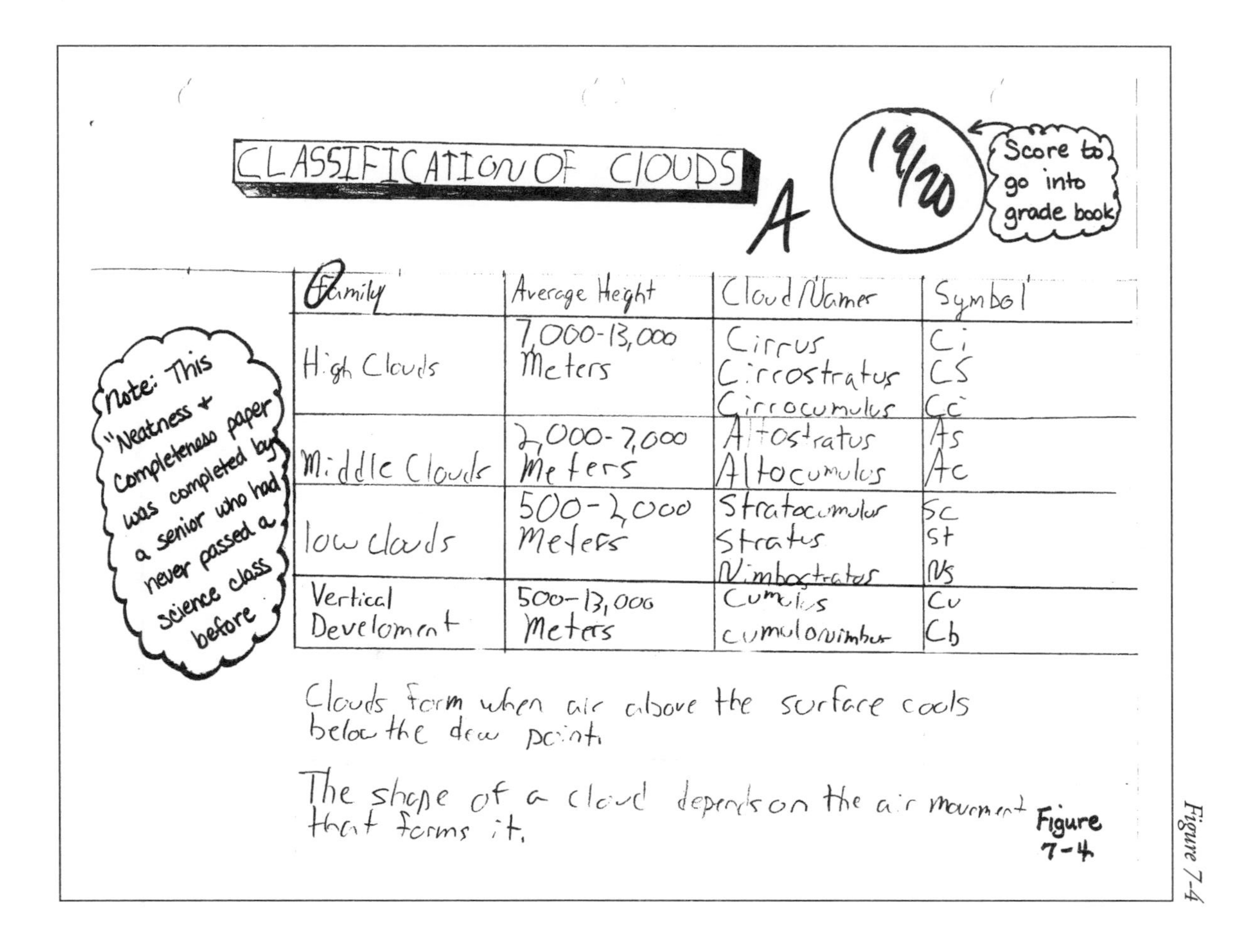

CLASSIFICATION OF CLOUDS

A

19/20

Score to go into grade book

Note: This "Neatness + Completeness paper was completed by a senior who had never passed a science class before

Family	Average Height	Cloud Names	Symbol
High Clouds	7,000-13,000 Meters	Cirrus Cirrostratus Cirrocumulus	Ci Cs Cc
Middle Clouds	2,000-7,000 Meters	Altostratus Altocumulus	As Ac
low clouds	500-2,000 Meters	Stratocumulus Stratus Nimbostratus	Sc St Ns
Vertical Develoment	500-13,000 Meters	Cumulus cumulonimbus	Cu Cb

Clouds form when air above the surface cools below the dew point.

The shape of a cloud depends on the air movment that forms it.

Figure 7-4

Summary

In the previous chapters, I have tried to share with you how I came to this place in my professional journey. I have also shared with you "tricks of the trade."

People often ask me what I like best about teaching. First, I really like working with young people. To earn money for college, I baby-sat three years for a family with six children. The Mom and Dad of this family paid me for working eleven to thirteen hours a day. That meant *I* was with the children during their waking hours more than their parents! I figured if I still enjoyed working with young people after that, I should choose a profession that involved that love. I have never regretted my decision.

Second, I really enjoy the creative freedom we have in our classrooms. Sure, we have a lot of demands on what we need to teach, but HOW we teach it is still mostly a product of our creativity. I hope the ideas and suggestions in this first section have at least given you *some* ideas to modify and fit into your teaching style, thus reducing your fatigue, while increasing student responsibility.

This concludes PART I. See if you feel comfortable with the concepts associated with these 28 key words or phrases:

- Imagineering
- Early Work
- WIIFM
- 100% attention
- Skeleton Schedule
- Quality Standard Bonus
- *Mystery of Life*
- Change of test focus
- Sleep Deprivation
- Levels of Competency
- Helping or enabling

- Responsibility moving-overmanship
- Butcher paper schedule
- Two uses for Rubbermaid tubs
- Personal Grade Book (PGB)
- Parentally maintained or parentally socialized
- Class dismissal routine
- *Teacher Prowl*
- In-class breaks
- Using color
- Lots of points
- Late work philosophy
- Using the overhead for instructions
- Using the overhead to share test grades
- Using the overhead to correct papers together
- Neatness and completeness
- Colored folders for teachers
- Go vertical with class sets of papers

Part I of this book has been designed to provide responsibility management skills, time management skills and paper management skills. It is my hope that these techniques have helped to reduce teacher stress and fatigue, while giving specific techniques for increasing student responsibility for their own learning. Once the stress and fatigue have been at least lessened, I hope you will feel energetic enough to read Part II.

Part II of this book will deal with specific new techniques researched from the business community, from Dr. Deming, and from David Langford's *Quality Learning Seminars*. These activities have dramatically reduced the number of behavior problems occurring in my classes AND have developed higher level thinking skills in students, while *reducing* my paper correction and general stress load. These activities have also brought more positive feedback from parents, administrators and students than I ever experienced before. I hope they will do the same for you!

When you are ready, read Part II for some hints on TRUE systemic change that does *not cost much money* and actually *increases the use of higher level thinking skills* while *reducing your paper correcting and behavior modification duties!*

Notes, *Part I*

Notes, *Part I*

part two

Systemic change in the way we
"do business" in the classroom
can be done with less work for teachers
and for no additional cost to school districts

CHAPTER 8

Activities and Games to begin the *Teaching Smarter* classroom and to build team skills

In the classrooms of the past, where students sat passively in chairs facing the front of the room, it was not unusual for students to spend an entire semester in a class and not know the name of the person sitting three chairs behind them. As we move into the classrooms of the future, we are focusing more on active processing and teamwork. It is vital that EVERYONE in the class know the name of the rest of the people in the class. One cannot function well in a team if they do not know the names of the people they are working with.

During the first few days of setting up a *Teaching Smarter* environment, we spend time getting to know the people we will be working with.

Here are a few ideas to get you started.

Pipe Cleaner Introductions—Students are paired. Each person has three minutes to interview their partner. Students are encouraged to take notes. After the six minute total, each student is given a pipe cleaner to shape into a symbol for their new friend. Then pairs are called up at random (you may choose to ask for volunteers at first) to introduce their new friend to the class.

By using pipe cleaners, we bypass the "I have no art talent" phobia. The students usually display a full range, from abstract shapes because their new friend is a complicated person, to the letter "C" because my new friend's name is Carol.

This activity is very successful. Our young friends like to hear about their peers! The pipe cleaner adds that little extra that makes it different from "Tell us a little bit about yourself." The fact that they are introducing someone else seems to help even the shy people get up in front of the class.

The Walk Around—Before starting the interviews, I usually do what I call a "Walk Around." I ask each person to write down three interview questions they might ask. Then we go around the room and each person reads one item from their list. If one already has that question, they just put a check by it. If one does not already have the question, they add it to their list. As ideas are said, I write them on the overhead. A student has the right to say "pass" if all their ideas have already been said by the time we get to them. This activity assures each person has several questions to ask during their three minute interview. Students do not HAVE to use these questions, but it really helps the shy or insecure person.

I usually do no more than fifteen introductions during one period. Most classes will take no more than two days to finish. There is usually laughter, and a feeling of knowing one another really sets a pleasant tone for the class.

Teacher Introduction— AFTER we finish the STUDENT introductions, I introduce myself. I bring pictures of my family and share a little bit about myself as a person. Then I share about myself as a professional. "How do we know that the mechanic we take our car to is a professional? We see the papers on the wall telling of all the courses s/he has taken to become knowledgeable about cars. How do we know the doctor we go to when we are sick is trained well enough to take care of us? We can see the framed degrees on the wall of the waiting room. And yet, when we come to school, how do we know that the teacher is knowledgeable about teaching? I want to share with you the papers that show I have the training and education to be your teacher."

Then I pass around my framed high school diploma. Sure, it's old, but they do not change much, and many of our students know they are working towards a high school diploma, but they have never SEEN one. I follow the high school diploma with my Associate of Arts degree, my Bachelor of Arts degree, my Master of Education degree and the certificate from the state that permits me to teach. I also let them know that I have an additional 90 credits (or two years) of college courses focused on learning theories. I think it's important for our students to know they are now working with the most educated group of people some of them will ever have the privilege of working closely with. Even if they go on to college and work with educated people, **they may never again work with so many educated people whose sole reason for being there is to help them get better!**

Here's an interesting idea, rather than wearing our college gowns only at graduation, how about wearing them also on the first day of school? That would *certainly* set a visual mind set for the educational level of the people who manage the classrooms!

If you have not framed your degrees, please do so. I know for the first several years my degrees were in an envelope in a file cabinet at home. We worked hard for those degrees. Celebrate your accomplishments. Frame the papers and put them on a wall in your home. Then once a year, pack them up and take them to school for "show and tell." One of the teachers in one of my seminars said she was going to take the degrees to Kinko and have copies made so she could hang the papers on the wall in her classroom. Hey, if it's good enough for doctors and mechanics and lots of other well trained people, it should be good enough for us too!

Class Seating Chart—In the classroom of the past, the teacher had a seating chart, but the students did not. In a *Teaching Smarter* classroom, ALL people of the class have a seating chart. We create it together. I do a seating chart on the overhead, and students do their own seating chart oriented to where they are seated. I spell the names (first and last) with the help of the student. Sometimes I demonstrate how to also spell a name phonetically, if it is difficult to pronounce correctly. After all, one of the sweetest sounds we hear is someone else saying our name—CORRECTLY. Students are further encouraged to know their peers' names when I explain a 25 point extra credit opportunity. In order to earn the 25 extra credit points, a student needs to stand up and say the first and last name of each person in the room without looking at the seating chart. The window of opportunity is the first two weeks of class. Since I structure lots of points in my class, 25 points is not a huge influence on grades, but it does raise the interest in knowing names. Even the students who choose not to stand up and say first and last names are learning as they watch their peers stand up and attempt to say every name with not one error.

Who's Missing?—If you have a few minutes, this is a quick and easy name game to play. One person leaves the room. One person hides. The first person comes back in the room and tries to guess "Who's missing?" To complicate the game, have one person leave the room, one person hides, and everyone else switches seats! This makes the game much harder, as can be seen on the face of the person who returns to the room to guess "Who's Missing?"

The Debrief—REMEMBER, IF IT IS IMPORTANT, WE SPEND TIME ON IT. The students know this intuitively. It's not what we SAY that is important, it is what we spend time on that is perceived as really important.

Students love to play games in the classroom. Most of them consider it a diversion from learning, with no homework! It is our job to use games as a learning tool AND to share the *purpose* of the game with the students. That way if the student goes home and is asked, "What did you do in school today?" the student does not reply, "We got to waste some time playing games." That is not good public relations for schools!

I have developed a pattern for using games which has been very successful in helping students see the *purpose* for the game.

First, always give the rules for the game in the classroom while students are seated. It is more fun to play the game outside, but we will never have better attention than we have in the classroom. Tell the students you will give the rules twice—then you will ask for questions. Once the game begins, the teacher will *only* give information that was not given in the classroom, other information must be obtained from classmates. It is sometimes hard not to answer a student's question, but we are building reliance on peers with this rule—and freeing ourselves of endlessly answering the same questions over and over.

After the game is completed, it is critical to debrief the *purposes* of the game. The debrief is done back in the classroom. Students will not usually process the purpose without a debrief. The debrief may only last for five minutes or less, but it is a critical step. The debrief is so critical that IF THERE IS NOT TIME TO DEBRIEF, DO NOT PLAY THE GAME.

As teachers, we think of games, or other forms of skill practice, as complete learning experiences in and of themselves. However, while students are participating in an exercise, their minds are often filled with thoughts that are necessary for making the exercise productive (otherwise known as "winning"). Their thoughts are not related to the learning objectives of the exercise. They are probably concentrating on performing correctly or following the rules. Some students are focused on others' behavior. Still others are coping with stresses from outside the classroom.

Therefore, directly after an experientially rich or complex activity, the students have only *begun* to learn from it. DEBRIEFING is the process of pinpointing, revealing, and applying meaningful lessons from an activity.

Debriefing frequently will include such things as:

- Venting Emotions—this step allows students to release feelings so they are not distracted as the activity is processed
- Sharing Insights—students reflect on general insights, with very little help from the leader
- Determining Behaviors—leader helps students convert general insights to specific beneficial behaviors or ideas
- Transferring Behaviors—students apply the learnings to their own world, they make it personal
- Suggesting Improvements—the best time to do quality improvement on the activity is directly after it has taken place

In the following several pages I will give you the first few games I use at the start of the school year, or when I begin *Teaching Smarter* techniques. There is nothing like playing games to set the stage for "Something different is happening in this class." By using the debrief, students can go home at night and talk about *what* they did in school and *why* they did it. In this way parents understand the games were a learning experience and FUN (neat huh?).

GAME 1
The Name Game

Materials needed: one small stuffed animal and a stopwatch or clock with a second hand

---

In order to build a team feeling, it is important to know each other's names. In the "regular" classroom, the teacher spends a lot of effort learning the students' names in the first few days. However, it is not uncommon for students to be unaware of most classmates' names, even at the end of a semester! We cannot expect students to work together when they do not even know the names of their coworkers.

If you choose to play these games the first few days of class, the students will be learning names right along with you. I have found that their empathy is directly proportional to their *own* experience. Students are more forgiving of my not knowing *their* name if they themselves are struggling with learning all the names.

The first day I play a very simple game. The students are still rather shy, since they don't know everyone in the class. If at all possible, go outside to play the game. I've had students say, "Outside? I haven't had recess in years!" They love going outside. This will really help make them believers that something different is happening in this classroom.

Rules for the first game:

"When I give the signal word, I want you to go outside to the ____area." (Try to pick a place close by, but not too near other classes, be courteous or some teachers *will* complain.)

"When we get to the location, form one large circle, each person should be able to just barely stretch their arms to touch the shoulder of the person next to them."

"I will give someone this stuffed animal." (Hold up a small, about fist-sized, stuffed animal. I get mine from the local thrift store for about 25 cents each. I suggest you not use one of your children's toys. If someone gets "cute" and drops it in a puddle, or otherwise damages it, you do not want any personal connection to the toy.)

"The task is to throw the toy across the circle and say the receiving person's name *loudly* so we can all hear and begin to know the person's name. It is OK to point to the person and ask their name if you do not know it. There are lots of us, myself included, who do not know many names yet. The new person then throws the toy back *across* the circle to a new person and says the new name loudly so we can all hear and begin to know the person's name. We will continue until all people have received the toy. The last person throws the toy back to the original person." (Hint, I use the following technique to keep track of who has received the toy and who has not—hands in front ready to catch the toy if you have NOT received the toy, hands in back if you HAVE received the toy.)

"Be sure to say the receiver's name LOUDLY. We are *all* trying to learn the names."

"Toss the toy underhanded. It is friendlier and easier to catch than an overhand throw."

Do a couple of demonstrations in the classroom.

"We will do this activity for three rounds. Each round you will throw the toy to the same person you threw it to the first time, saying their name loudly so we can all hear. The second and third time I will use a stopwatch to time you. The goal is to complete the task in as little time as possible." (Repeat the rules quickly one more time.)

"Are there any questions? OK, let's go outside and play!"

During my years as an elementary teacher, I taught kindergarten for two of the thirteen years. I was taught by an experienced pre-school teacher that there are MANY things one can learn by watching children at play. The same is true in higher grades. The first day you will see relationships, leadership, shyness and aggression in ways that may never show up in the classroom, at least not right away. You will also share in laughter, the sweet music of using games for learning!

After returning to the classroom, put a piece of plastic on the overhead and write the word "DEBRIEF" at the top. Ask the students, "Why did I take precious class time to go outside and play? How could I educationally justify this activity to the principal?"

They will come up with such things as "to learn names, to work together, to get to know each other." Be sure and offer positive feedback. These are your "brave" students— the ones who are willing to speak up the first day of class.

I then seize the "teachable moment." We talk about how the first game teaches the foundation rules for how we play games in this class. In addition, we are learning about what a debrief is.

> I also talk to them about endorphins, the natural high. "Endorphins are the body chemical released by exercise, and by laughter. It has been shown that a person in the hospital will recover faster if the friends and family who visit help them laugh. We do not know why, but endorphins seem to aid in healing. Likewise, people who laugh together, feel more friendly towards each other, are less likely to be mean to each other and can work more cooperatively together. We will be doing group work in this class and I want you to feel comfortable in the classroom and with each other. So, when you go home tonight and someone asks you what you did in school today, tell them you played a game designed to learn names and produce endorphin release for building team cooperation. It will sound real important—AND IT IS, EVEN THOUGH IT WAS FUN TOO!"

GAME 2

Bears In The Air

Materials needed: About a dozen small animals in a paper sack and a stopwatch or clock with a second hand

---

The next class day I play "Bears in the Air." This game builds on the first game. Here's what I say to the students:

> "Today we are going to play a game that starts out like the game we played last time." (Here I review the rules from last time.)
>
> - Introduce the game in the classroom,
> - give the rules twice,
> - model what we want (be sure to EMPHASIZE the underhanded throw),
> - and ask for questions before going outside.
>
> "This time you may choose a different person across the circle." (You see, the students tend to stand in the circle with their friends next to them. This almost guarantees that the person across the circle will be new to them.)
>
> "Remember, try to learn as many new names as you can."
>
> "After three rounds, I will complicate the game. I will not tell you what the more complex way is at this time. Are there any questions? Let's go outside and play!"

Just like yesterday, we go outside and they form a circle. The first three rounds go very quickly. During the first round, be sure and remind students to put "hands in front if you have not had the stuffed animal, hands in back if you have. Toss the stuffed animal to the SAME person every time and say their name LOUDLY."

After three rounds, reach into the bag you have brought out, but kept sealed. I usually use a paper bag or a dark plastic bag with a draw string that I get from a local retail store. Inside the bag are about a dozen more little stuffed animals.

As we begin round number four, I whisper to the start person, "I'm going to hand you some more animals. Wait until the person you threw to has tossed the first animal to the next person and said the name. Then call their name out *again* as you toss *another* animal." (About every five seconds, hand the starter another animal. Soon there are all kinds of animals flying in all kinds of directions, stuffed animals collide in mid-air, students are dropping toys, students are getting hit in the head with stuffed piggies and doggies, and even the most shy person is laughing.)

As the animals come back to the starter, the animal is handed to you and replaced in the bag. When the last animal is in the bag, the game is over and you all return to the room for the debrief.

In the classroom, once again, take out a sheet of plastic, write the word "DEBRIEF" at the top and display it on the overhead.

> "Why did I take time from our precious class time to play a game? How could I educationally justify this game if my boss were to walk in?"

By now you should be receiving some more spontaneous responses—students are starting to feel more comfortable.

If students do not bring it up on their own, ask them about that scientific word we talked about yesterday. You know, the one that begins with "e." That's right "endorphins." Also, ask them why you chose to use stuffed animals and not rubber balls.

> "That's right, the purpose of this game is not throwing and catching, so I wanted to use objects that were soft (if they hit you) and objects that would not bounce away if dropped or if a catch is missed."

After you have recorded the list from students on the overhead, explain that there was another goal that you had, in addition to the ones the students already identified. "I want you to think about all the things in your life that require time and attention. Think about things like school, friends, work, sports, your car, your family, your boy/girl friend. Each of these things have demands on your time, but are not beyond your ability to handle—one at a time. However, think about the game we just played. Was throwing a stuffed animal underhand and saying someone's name a hard task? Was catching a stuffed animal a hard task? So, what made the task so difficult in the last round?" (The students usually quickly come up with something about the number and speed with which the toys kept coming.)

> "That's right, sometimes it is not the *difficulty* of the tasks that make your life stressful, it is just the *number of them* coming at you all at once! If we have too many "Bears in the Air" in our LIFE, the same thing happens. Our skill level goes down, we miss really easy things, our stress goes up and we make mistakes. Unfortunately, the fun part is not present—like in our game—it is just *very* stressful. One of the ways to manage that stress, is to *intentionally* drop a 'bear' or two, get in control, then pick up the 'bear(s)' again."

"For example, my daughter was a senior in high school. She was taking two classes at the local community college, two classes at her local high school and a sports medicine class at a neighboring high school. In addition, she was working at an espresso stand twenty hours a week, and playing as a starter on a rugby team that practiced 20 miles away. Then one of the espresso stand people quit, and my daughter was working thirty hours a week. One night she came home and started just sobbing. 'I'm so stressed out! All I feel like doing is crying all the time.' Well, she had too many 'Bears in the Air.' It took quite some time to convince her that she needed to drop one or two things. You see, she didn't start out doing all those things at once. They were added on, one at a time, but nothing was dropped! The next thing she knew—life was incredibly busy! It was hard, but she decided to drop out of Rugby for the rest of the semester and cut back on her espresso stand hours. Was it easy? No. However, something *had* to be intentionally dropped or everything would suffer.

On a side note, when my daughter told her espresso boss that her Mom said she had to cut her hours back to twenty a week or quit her job—THE BOSS FOUND A NEW EMPLOYEE WITHIN A FEW DAYS! Sometimes when we practically kill ourselves trying to help a system, the system is not motivated to solve our problem. After all, now it is *our* problem, not the system's problem. We, in essence have solved the system's problem! The system is no longer in crisis, so it is not motivated to change." (Hmmmm, as teachers, we need to think about that!)

"There will be times this year when you will have too many 'Bears in the Air.' You will need to intentionally drop a thing or two, to pick up later (or maybe not). You will *not* be doing your best quality work if you try to handle *everything* all the time."

This is a great game for lessons of life. Students will come up to me during the year. I can tell they are stressed out. It really helps them to be able to say, "Mrs. LaBelle, I have too many 'Bears in the Air!' I have got to drop something."

Teachers too—We need to realize when WE have too many "Bears in the Air."

Recognizing a problem is the first step toward solution!
Or, as the business world would say:
A problem well defined is a problem half-solved!

GAME 3
Get the Time Down

Materials: one small stuffed animal and a stop watch or clock with a second hand

This game starts out the same way as the first two games. However, once we are all outside, and have done the first three rounds, the instructor gives these additional instructions:

> "Listen carefully. I will repeat these instructions two times, and two times only. You are allowed to ask questions after that. I will only answer questions that were not already addressed in the instructions. If the answer has already been given, I will ask you to consult with your peers. Please listen carefully."
>
> "The stuffed animal MUST touch peoples' hands in the same order. Your task now is to get the time down as far as you can. As you recall, when we played this game before, I timed the group. Do you remember what the best time was? The task now is to improve on that time. After you finish, I will share with you what other groups have been able to reduce the time to."

It is sometimes difficult, but this is where the teacher just gets out of the way! Stand back and do your best to only speak when spoken to. This is a great chance to really begin seeing the problem-solving potential of your group, who takes leadership, who has great ideas (but is perhaps not listened to), who is shy, who is outgoing, etc.

Ask anyone who has played the game before to be an experienced observer. Ask them to make silent notes to themselves for sharing during the debrief. I have found it helps to point out that solving a puzzle for someone is like the Easter Egg hunt where the older child points out all the hiding spots for the younger child, because the younger child is not yet wise enough to find the eggs on their own. "Let your friends discover the solution.

They are not dumb, and they do not need your help. There is much more pleasure in solving the puzzle, than in being told the answer!"

The students will eventually figure out that the instructions did not mention anything about saying names, after the first three rounds. They will probably try rearranging the circle so people can pass the toy to the person next to them. Many groups decide to stand in a straight line, hold out their hands and have the starter RUN down the line.

The fastest way (and all the groups have eventually found it) is to stand in order closely and in a circle, hold out a hand, and have the starter pivot around with the toy touching all the hands in order. The time is below two seconds.

The instructor usually will have to encourage more creative solutions the first few times by simply saying, "You can do better!" They do not believe more reduction is possible at first.

During the debrief, back at the classroom, there should be lots of input by now. Allow students to make as long a list as they can.

At the end I add this part:

> "Has anyone ever seen this word before?" (Write the word, "paradigm" on the overhead. If they have seen it before—great, have the students define it. If not, write the definition on the overhead.
>
> In either case, have the students write the word and definition in their notebooks. Be sure they can pronounce "pair—a—dime.")
>
> "A paradigm is an accepted way of thinking or of doing things. Many paradigms come about as 'just the way we have always done things, and there's no need for change now!' at least for some people."
>
> "There was a new wife who was going to serve ham for the couple's first family holiday dinner. As she was preparing the meat, she cut the ends off the ham. 'Honey,' her husband asked, 'why are you cutting off pieces of the ham?'

The new wife replied, 'Because my Mom is a great cook, and she always cut the ends off the ham. I think it is so the juices can flow better.'

During dinner, the new husband asked the new Mother-in-law why she always cut the ends off her hams. 'Oh that,' the lady said, 'I had this great pan that cooked meat really well. However, when we had company, I had to buy the biggest ham possible, and usually I bought it a little large—so I had to trim the ends off.'

"Without knowing it, a paradigm had been formed, and a reason was made up that seemed to justify it. Until the young wife heard it from her Mom, do you think her husband could have encouraged her to take the risk, and NOT cut the ends off the ham?"

"All of us have paradigms in our life. I am going to ask you to push on your comfort level a bit from time to time. Before you played the game, if I had shared with you the goal of "all hands will touch the stuffed animal *in order* in two seconds or less," many of you would have thought, 'Mrs. LaBelle you have been teaching TOO LONG. It's time to retire. There is no way we can do that!' However, you would have been thinking of the game within the old paradigm. As you now know, it is very possible—it just required thinking a little differently about the task. I promise you, I will never ask you to do anything, unless I KNOW YOU CAN DO IT."

Many employers today are involved in paradigm shifts regarding how they manage and how they conduct business. IT'S IMPORTANT THAT WE KNOW PARADIGM SHIFTS ARE SCARY AND MAY SEEM IMPOSSIBLE AT FIRST—BUT IF WE THINK CREATIVELY IT IS POSSIBLE."

GAME 4
People Puzzles

Materials: one 12" piece of clothesline for each student

This game can easily be played in the classroom or outside, but it is better received if you can "go outside and play." Students are grouped before going outside. The groups need to be about 8 to 10 people each. This will form three or four groups per class. For this game it is best to give instructions while students are standing in the grouped circles.

Here's what I say to the students:

> "Today we are going to play a totally different game. Each of you is holding a short length of rope. Please put the rope in your right hand.
>
> Offer the other end of your rope to a person across the circle. Make sure each rope is connected to a different person.
>
> There should now be a grid (or spider web) of rope in the center of the circle.
>
> Each time you talk to someone during the game, you must *say their name first.* If someone talks to you without saying your name first, you need to say, 'What's my name?' If the person does not know your name, *someone else* in the group can help them. YOU should not tell YOUR name. Do not respond to a person's instruction unless they first say your name.
>
> Without letting go of your rope, the task is to untangle the ropes.
>
> This is not a race. When the first group finishes the task, turn your ropes in to me. Then your job is to go over to other groups, observe and offer help, *if they ask for it.* Otherwise, your job is to observe and think of things to contribute during the debrief."

Once all groups have finished, it is time to return to the classroom and debrief.

You know the drill, "Why did I take valuable class time to play a game? How could I educationally support this activity to my boss?"

By now the students have a pattern going, and there should be no problem getting responses.

Besides the reasons similar to the previous games, there is one conclusion I want them to arrive at for sure. This game focused on teamwork and group support. The idea of one winner, and several losers does not support teamwork. The old way provides only ONE winner person or group. In the old way, losers *always* outnumber the winners. It is only a pleasant experience for a minority.

This game was different in the way it recognized the first team to finish. To finish first was not to win, but to become the assistants, if asked to help, to the other groups. All groups won, some just faster than others. There are more times in today's work world where teamwork is required, rather than a need for one winner and lots of losers.

For example, those of us who have children know there is a great variety in the ages at which children learn to walk. Walking at eight months or at fourteen months really does not matter by the time a child enters school. There are many things where it is important to learn well, but not necessarily important to learn first. Those who learn later are not dumber, they just need more time. The important thing is that we all learn.

I will never forget when my son was a senior in high school. He was a wrestler. He was undefeated throughout the entire season, all through the playoffs, right up until the final match of the state tournament. The final match was between my son and another undefeated wrestler. It was the match of the evening with lots of crowd attention. My son lost in overtime by one point. As I watched him on the platform, standing in second place, having his picture taken and fighting back tears, the Mommy part of me was hurting right along with him. However, I was still taken aback when my husband and I congratulated him on a great season, and his reply was,

"You're supposed to say that, you're my parents. But everyone else thinks I'm a loser!"

My friends, we cannot continue to support a mind set of one winner and *lots* of losers.

Of course, there *are* some times where one needs to be first to win (like in a business bid for a contract), but there are many more times where being first carries the responsibility of helping others be successful too. That's called teamwork.

Teamwork is where we work together
for success with dignity for all who try.

also

The early bird may get the worm—but the second mouse gets the cheese *(Being first is not always the best)*

or

TOGETHER
EVERYONE
ACCOMPLISHES
MORE

CHAPTER 9

Where Did *Teaching Smarter* Come From?

Now that you are using the methods outlined in PART I, I hope you are feeling more relaxed and organized and ready for more suggestions. The ideas I shared with you in the first section are responsibility, time and classroom management ideas I developed and used successfully in my classrooms for over 30 years. However, these methods were not enough as the school system moved into teaching the higher level thinking skills, creating new curriculum, integrating learning and using group situations more often. I found myself, once again, trying harder and stealing more and more time from my family and from my personal time. Having gone through this once before, you would think I would have learned!

I am reminded of the teachings in psychology pointing out that when one is under extreme stress, it is normal to revert to old behavior habits. That is why the person who was abused as a child, will vow never to abuse their kids. However, under the stress of financial problems, child rearing and relationship problems, what happens? That's right, the old patterns emerge "automatically" and the person abuses their kids. The very thing they swore they would never do. The same is true for substance addiction, or other destructive behavior patterns. Many of us, myself included, suffer from the self-abuse problem of responding to job stress by becoming single focused, by trying to teach better through working harder and longer. However, awareness is the most powerful tool for prevention. BE AWARE AND THINK *DEVIANTLY* ABOUT HOW TO TEACH!

The second time I began to be under tremendous stress, something else happened I did not expect. Not only did I "automatically" go into "rob from my home life" mode, but my body began to have physical problems MUCH faster! It was like my body said to itself, "Oh, I remember this. When under this much stress, we have bad headaches, muscle tension, digestive problems and sleep problems." In a strange way, I guess that was good. Good, because I realized quickly that "something different must be done if I am going to stay in the profession I love."

I decided to think deviantly and step out of teaching to look for answers. We are managers of people. We conduct "meetings" on a daily basis. We have to manage difficult people, and communicate with unhappy customers at times. These are all problems experienced in the business workplace, and just like us, they hold seminars and workshops on how to do their job better. Why not see if I could find some fresh ideas in the business world and modify them for more efficient teaching? (Like I said before, I'm not the most creative person, but I have a lot of experience with a wide variety of learners. And, I *can* modify well!)

I took Fred Pryor Workshops. (The phone number is 1-800-255-6139.) These are one day, intensive workshops. I would walk out of these workshops with a handbook and a drained feeling, like after a really hard final. Here are some of the titles you might be interested in.

- Conflict Management and Confrontational Skills
- How to Supervise People
- How to Transform Marginal Employees Into Solid Performers
- How to Become a Great Communicator
- How to Organize and Maintain Files and Records

There are many more, but you get the idea. These workshops focus on specific things one can do. I leave these workshops with ideas for me and with ideas for helping students.

Believe me, once you take *one* of their workshops you will receive PLENTY of informational fliers on a regular basis! The price is reasonable and the workshops are given in big cities nation wide.

Another source I turned to for ideas was my husband. He works as a manager for the Boeing Company and regularly checks out self improvement and management audio tapes from the tape library. Since he has to travel about an hour each way to work, he uses the time to "get smarter." He calls it "diamond mining" because, "You gotta go through a lot of stuff before you get something really good." I benefit from his research in many ways, not the least of which is that he listens to *all* these different tapes, then recommends the "jewels" for me to listen to. This is great, because he listens to some real "dogs" and all *I* have to do is listen to him gripe! However, I have to say he has saved me HOURS of wasted time. We also discuss the tapes after we have both listened to them. In this way I am able to process new information by listening *and* through discussion.

I want to make some recommendations to you, my new friend. Hopefully, you will find some time to listen to these people on tape. Most of these tapes can be checked out, or ordered, from your public library. It is recommended that one listen to a tape *at least* three times to *begin* making them part of their thinking. I'm going to give you a brief summary to help you make your first choice.

Bill Onckin: *Managing Management Time* or *"Who's got the monkey?*

This tape series will have you laughing as you learn! That's why I recommend it for your first experience. Mr. Onckin does a wonderful job of describing how we all tend to "naturally" manage in a way that causes us unnecessary toil and trouble. He refers to problems as "monkeys who need regular feeding and watering." For example, he claims one can always tell an inexperienced or ineffective manager, because if one walks into their office, "monkeys" are *everywhere* in various stages of neglect. This happens, he says, because the manager thinks no one can care for "monkeys" as well as he or she can. The result, the office is FULL of "monkeys." There are so many "monkeys" the boss is overwhelmed. Sound familiar? Even if it's not *you*, I'll bet you know someone like this! According to Mr. Onckin, the effective manager MONITORS the care and feeding of "monkeys", but does not DO it all. Throughout the tape series, Bill Onckin continues this mental picture technique. You will chuckle and learn—I guarantee it! If you have trouble finding the tape series, there is a book by Bill Onckin that addresses the same subject. I just learn better by hearing it.

Steven Covey: *The Seven Habits of Highly Effective People*

This is a BASIC for most business graduates. Although Mr. Covey is not as entertaining as Bill Onckin, the tapes are easy to listen to and provide some very helpful hints on how to live your life well. You will probably find some ideas worth sharing with students. Most tape series will include a booklet, for the visual learners.

Jim Rohn: *The Art of Exceptional Living*

This series is also easy to listen to and humorous. Jim Rohn has a distinctive voice he uses in the live audience portion of the tapes. It is interesting to listen to the two different voices of Jim Rohn. These tapes will help you journey further down the road of thinking for self preservation and improvement in all areas of life.

These are only a few suggestions. I suggest you go to your local library and do a little "diamond mining" of your own. As lifelong learners, it is quite a growth experience!

In addition to the business workshops and the audio tapes, I took David Langford's *Quality Learning Seminar*—two times. (Hey, I never said I was a FAST learner!) David Langford was a teacher who studied the philosophies of Dr. Deming as part of his master's degree. After Dr. Deming, David's life was changed forever. Soon after implementing the Deming "modified by Langford for education" ideas into the classroom, David was away from his classroom a lot to teach the techniques to other teachers. Due to popular demand, David Langford now is a full time international consultant, and lives on a 100 acre ranch in Montana. (If you would like to take a *Quality Learning Seminar*, you can get more information by calling 406-245-7773)

I also did research on business world management ideas through books and magazines. One whole summer was devoted to "how can I stay in teaching, teach to higher level thinking skills AND stay healthy and happy in my profession?"

The work-in-progress final product is what I call *Teaching Smarter.*

Experience teaches nothing without theory. Do not try to copy someone else's successes—unless you understand the theory behind it.
—W. Edwards Deming

I will keep the philosophy light and the practicalities heavy. However, when things go wrong, and we know they occasionally will, philosophy helps us know how to modify the lesson for success.

When you decide to try this method, *share the philosophy with your students.* They need to know where this new stuff is coming from. Everything in this book is provided as suggestions. You use your wonderful creativity to modify the suggestions to fit your style, needs and subject matter.

OK, so here's how I would explain *Teaching Smarter* to the students. "I read a book about a new way of teaching. The new way is called *Teaching*

Smarter I want to share the ideas with you. First, the book says we need to change the *words* we use if we are going to change the way we look at things. So, the word 'teacher' is replaced with the words 'classroom manager' and the word 'student' is replaced with the words 'classroom worker.' I will probably slip up from time to time, but I know you will help me as we begin to change the way we 'do business' in this classroom." (A private note: You better believe they will "remind" you!)

"You will hear some people refer to *students* as the product of the schools. If we think this way, teachers work *on* students to try and make them smarter. The new way of thinking changes the thinking to 'The LEARNING is the product of the schools. The classroom managers and classroom workers *together* produce the best quality product (the learning) that they can.' In this new system, the classroom manager asks the classroom workers what *they* need to do the best job possible. It is then the classroom manager's job to access the school system, in ways the classroom workers cannot, and provide the 'tools' needed for the best quality product. This is a FUNDAMENTAL CHANGE. It is no longer the boss telling the workers what to do. It is no longer the boss thinking that s/he already knows what the workers need. It is now the *workers'* job to communicate to the manager what is needed to do a quality job. It is the manager's job to help the worker do the quality job by accessing the system in ways the worker cannot do."

"Many businesses are implementing this philosophy. After all, it is the worker who knows best what is needed to do the best job they can. It is the classroom manager's job to provide knowledge of the system and facilitate the needs of the worker. We will be making some decisions, as a group, for how this classroom will be run, and what you need and want. This is a *delegation* of power, not an abdication of leadership or responsibility." (A private note: I once heard this idea stated as "Allow the workers to do as they please—the manager simply narrows down the pleases!")

I then ask the students, "Please think about systems you have already experienced—your family system, your church system, your school system, your classroom systems, your friendship systems. There are people in every system called 'suboptimizers.' Someone who helps a system be its best is called an optimizer, so a suboptimizer is what?" The students quickly come up with a definition like, "someone who does not make a system its best." Or, better yet, "A suboptimizer is someone who actively tries to subvert, or make the system worse."

Then I ask students if they can think of why a person would do such a thing. They usually come up with reasons like, "because they have a lot of anger, maybe the system isn't treating them right, and because THEY WANT ATTENTION." I focus on the wanting attention reason. "People who want attention will get it at any cost. In the school system, this attention getting will usually result in an angry teacher, a loss of your learning time, and sometimes more homework, or time served after class is over." Hear WIIFM playing in the background?

I continue with, "In most systems, unless the system makes a *conscious* effort not to, the rules of the system are made in response to the 10% suboptimizers. You see, it has been researched and found that in most systems, 90% or more of the people are willing to cooperate and help the system get better. However, the system is so busy dealing with the 10% suboptimizers, that they rarely have time to allow the 90% to help! IN THIS CLASSROOM, THE SUBOPTIMIZERS WILL NOT RULE!" When I say that, I swear I can almost feel a sigh of relief from the class, and I know I can see it in many of their eyes. They all know, they have just never had it put into words before. Another strange thing, I guess it comes under the *Mystery of Life* category, even the students who are usually "trouble-makers" are quick to say that suboptimizers will not rule. This redefinition changes a classroom disrupter from the "hero rebel against the teacher" to the classroom stinker who is robbing us of class time and a good natured teacher. It changes the whole attitude. Now it's OK to not support the suboptimizing behavior. THERE'S MORE—READ ON.

MAKE STUDENTS *PART* OF THE SYSTEM, AND THEY ARE LESS LIKELY TO TRY AND SUBOPTIMIZE IT.

Share with classroom workers that you will be taking data from them before you make many of the major decisions for the class. You need to build trust by asking the first question on the first day. This would be the first Early Work question. (Remember the one used for modeling how we want the Early Work done?) The question I use is, "Why are you taking this class?" I offer them five options (just to make the data gathering easier).

" 1. To graduate
2. For college
3. Was told to
4. No other class in the schedule
5. I like it."

Once finished, they turn the paper in to the green box by the Teddy Bear. Now, here's a critical step. Ask a CLASSROOM WORKER to volunteer to take the papers out of the box and tell you what the results are. This is the first step in showing how the classroom manager and the classroom worker will function together to gather data. Couldn't you just collect the papers and read them out loud to the students, or tell them what the results are the next day? Yes, but a big part of this activity is the *process.* In fact, in many of the activities I will show you in this section, THE PROCESS IS AT LEAST AS IMPORTANT AS THE PRODUCT. So, now we have a classroom worker reading out the responses as I tally them on the overhead. The classroom is quiet without reminders. The classroom workers are very interested in what their peers have to say! In addition, there is no doubt that what is on the overhead, and what they told me are one and the same. Have you ever been asked for input, and then just seen the final answer? If the answer was not what you contributed, and not what any of your friends contributed, but matched what the leader wanted for the answer, didn't you suspect the data had been manipulated? In a *Teaching Smarter* activity, all data is collected in plain sight.

After you have posed a question, collected data and totaled data in plain sight, the final step is to post the data somewhere in the classroom. There are very few better things we can do to validate input than to display it in the classroom. Now, a *chart* does not have to be a big paper. When I display the "Why are you taking this class" data, I use a piece of 10" x 20" piece of butcher paper. (By the way, I use different colored butcher paper charts for each class. So, for example, all physics charts are green, all earth science charts are pink, etc.) The only rule of thumb is that the students who sit furthest away can read the data from their seat.

Remember, we value quality, so spend some time making a "pretty" chart out of the collected data. Always include the focus question and always keep the raw data. Explain to our young adults that we keep the raw data so there is never any doubt that the summary chart reflects the data. This is the beginning of "up front" management—and it is powerful! (See sample chart on figure 9-1 at the end of this chapter.)

This first data gathering activity is kept simple on purpose. I'm rarely surprised by the results—but that's OK. If I am right in my assumptions about the reasons students are taking a particular class, great. If I am not right, it is certainly better to find out early! For example, if the answers cluster in the number one, three or four range, I would be in trouble if I taught the class in a pre-college manner. Likewise, when students give data clustered around the number two response, I have something to fall back on when students ask why they have homework! What I do is motivated by the DATA collected from the workers. It works for business and it works in a classroom.

The Next Chapters

The next chapters will show you how to do consensus decision making—without taking all day. In my state, as in several others, we are working on

Figure 9-1

Charted results from 3 different subject areas in response to the question "Why are you taking this class?"

Why are you taking this class?
(2 Earth Science classes)

To graduate	44
For college	1
Was told to	7
No other class fit schedule	5
I like it	3

Why are you taking this class?
(1 Oceanography class)

To graduate	2
For college	5
Was told to	0
No other class fit schedule	3
I like it	18

Why are you taking this class
(2 Physics classes)

To graduate	0
For college	39
Was told to	2
No other class fit schedule	2
I like it	7

teaching to higher level thinking skills. We are developing activities in the classroom to promote those higher level thinking skills. Usually, this is where LOTS of teacher effort comes in. The activities I will share with you in the next few chapters will involve students in activities that:

- Help students set goals
- Encourage persistence
- Develop decision makers
- Encourage students to reflect, evaluate and ask questions
- Share information
- Show empathy and respect and peer encouragement
- Develop a high personal standard for work
- Reflect originality
- Base work on given criteria
- Encourage creativity and risk taking and
- Develop analytical problem solvers

ALL THIS WITH A *DECREASE* IN PAPERWORK AND A *DECREASE* IN PLANNING TIME! Sounds too good to be true? Read on.

CHAPTER 10

How to consisely lead classroom consensus decision making

Over the years, I have experienced different models for "site based decision making" or "consensus decision making" or whatever other name one might come up with for coming to a group agreement. Unfortunately, this was often interpreted as "everybody talks as *long* as they want until we can all agree on a decision." Those were some looooong staff meetings!

"Any decision that gets 100% agreement is either obvious or so watered down as to be worthless."—Connie Hoffman, *Putting Sense in Consensus*

In this chapter, I am going to introduce you to an activity that will be quick, needs very little planning and will bring a group of thirty to agreement within thirty-five to forty-five minutes, and usually *much* less. We will start out with the very easy and progress from there.

As I have mentioned earlier, I have a radio in my classroom. I went out and bought the BIGGEST boom box I could find. It has a radio, tape player and CD player. I wanted the biggest one I could find for under $100 (so I could be reimbursed by my school district). I realized ahead of time that little radios fit into book bags. It only takes one dishonest kid out of 150 to steal the radio and ruin my day. I have had this big boom box for four years now. Almost always, the classroom workers like to have the radio on during lab times or during book-work times. Of course, there is also almost always a disagreement as to what station the radio should be played. Here is a three minute way to decide:

- Give each student a small post-it note (I cut my larger ones up—just be sure there is a sticky part on each piece—found *that* out the hard way!)
- Without any discussion ask them to write the NUMBER of the station they would most like to listen to
- Then invite the classroom workers, row by row, or table by table, to bring their post-its to the front board
- If there is already a post-it with your station on it, just put your post-it under it to form a column
- If there is no other post-it with your numbers on it, begin a new column

Soon there will be an array of post-it columns. The longest three columns will be the stations listened to during work times. (There is a sample array on *figure 10-1* at the end of this chapter.) This whole process will take about three minutes the first time. Any time students want to re-vote, it's no big deal, and it will soon only take about 30 seconds. There is little to no argument, and the data is right there for all to see. I write the stations in pencil on the outside of the colored paper folder for each class. In this way I can erase if a re-vote changes the numbers. This is the second time you can obviously value student input. (The first time was the Early Work question, "Why are you taking this class?") The vote should be done within the first few days. By now you have asked and valued twice, thus supporting the claim that things will be done differently in this class.

This next activity is one of the most powerful tools you will be using. It is called the *Affinity Diagram*. In this activity, the classroom manager gathers data from the classroom workers and together, they categorize the responses and come to a group decision. The critical task for *you* is to create the focus question. After the classroom manager explains what a *Teaching Smarter* classroom is like, and what a suboptimizer is, it is time to involve students in an important class decision. I say to students, "We have talked about conscious competents, and how important it is to turn to your peers for help. I want you to be successful. I know you will be more successful if you can sit by friends. You realize, of course, that many teachers are not comfortable letting students sit by friends due to the actions of suboptimizers. Rather than ME telling YOU how to behave in this classroom, I believe it is time for the 90%+ to tell *me* what behaviors it is reasonable to expect in order for you to sit by friends. You have been in classes for a few years, you know what is appropriate. I am also aware that you are already making some very important decisions (For example, high school students are deciding whether or not to have sex, whether or not to drink, whether or not to drive responsibly.) Why would I not believe you can make decisions about appropriate behavior in the classroom?" After that build-up, I share the directions for how the decision will be made. "I will be showing you a focus question. Then I will ask you to form groups of five or six." (It's up to you. Sometimes I let students freely choose groups. Other times we use the counting or cards technique to randomly choose groups. You are the professional. After two or three days, you have a good idea of the maturity level of the class. If you have a large number of possible suboptimizers, it's best to use a random grouping activity, like numbering, or using cards. Otherwise, suboptimizers will group together and reinforce each other to subvert the activity.)

"I will give each group a stack of post-its. At the signal, I will show you the focus question, and you will have three silent minutes to do a 'silent brainstorm.' Many of us have done brainstorm activities before, the problem is that most of our communication is not verbal. It is visual. So if I roll my eyes (I demonstrate) when someone suggests an idea, I didn't need to SAY anything, but that person certainly got the negative response message!

With a 'silent brainstorm' you write three or four word responses to the focus question on the sticky note—one idea per sticky note. Write as many responses as you can think of in three minutes. Each person should have at least six sticky notes filled out by the end of three minutes. At the end of the three minutes I will have more instructions for processing the responses."

I usually pick the 6 or 12 on the clock as the second hand start point. The focus question is "What behaviors are reasonable for the teacher to expect in order for (name the class) students to sit by friends?" Notice the focus question is in stereo WIIFM. It has what *I* want and what the *students* will get.

"Ready?" I count down from "10, 9, 8...BEGIN." I pace the class at "one minute, half the time is over, thirty seconds to go, time is up." Once the time is up, I say, "STOP, now is the time to begin categorizing your table's responses. YOU are the only one to categorize YOUR post-it notes. Make columns, like you did for the radio station decision. *You* decide, for example, whether 'be quiet' means the same as 'no talking' as you group your sticky notes."

After a few minutes the tables have achieved the task. During this time the classroom manager tapes a large piece of butcher paper (about 3 feet x 8 feet) horizontally on the wall or board. The butcher paper has the focus question at the top.

Number the tables. Begin with "Table one, give me a category name for one of your categories." You write the category on the butcher paper. "All tables with post-it notes that would fit into this category, send someone up to put the notes on the butcher paper." Once all the tables have brought up their sticky notes for that category, draw a circle around the category, and move on to Table 2. "Table 2 give me another category that you made up." Continue until all post-its are on the butcher paper. Sometimes you will get notes like, "Smoke pot" or "Have sex." This is simply the suboptimizer testing you. Say something like, "This method values all input. I will never throw away your input" Then mark a circle at the bottom corner of the butcher paper and title it "Suboptimizer Comments." Invite the suboptimizer to put the post-its in the right place. Often, I will have students say, "Never mind." Expect to have some suboptimizer comments for the first few times. It is just a test. As soon as it becomes obvious that you are sincere, the suboptimizer contributions will cease. There is simply no glory in it!

I have found that post-it notes do not stick to butcher paper all that well. After a category is done. I take long strips of scotch tape and run it down the columns. With this method, the post-its will stay for an entire year! After all classes of the same subject have done the *Affinity Diagram*, it is time for the teacher to make a neat poster listing the focus question at the top, followed by the categories suggested by each class. I do not list like categories more than once. For example, "Be Responsible" and "Act Responsibly" would be only listed as one category. The instructor can also suggest modified category names during the charting activity. The finished product is a "Behavior Contract" developed *by* students, *for* students. Each year I have done this activity, "be responsible" is one of the biggest categories. This is true for all ability level classes. (See *figure 10-2* for a sample sketch of two *Affinity Diagrams* used to develop the "Behavior Contracts.")

The next time we have class together, I share the "Behavior Contract." The "Behavior Contract" is on a colored piece of butcher paper. (I use different colored charts for each different subject I teach. This reduces confusion as to which set of charted data belongs to which subject areas. If possible, physically separate the posters. For example, I put all physics data on green charts on the east wall, all earth science data on blue charts on the west wall and all oceanography data on pink charts on the south wall.) I have spent some time on this chart to make it neat. After all, it will be on the wall for the entire time the class meets in this room. The chart shows all the categories students created last time we were together. The "Behavior Contract" is taped to the wall, with the sticky-noted *Affinity Diagrams* under it. This is called "poster stacking" and it is a wonderful way to get lots of material on the wall. Students do not need to see the *whole* poster, just enough to be a reminder. It is important to put the *Affinity Diagrams* behind the "Behavior Contract" because the post-its provide the "definition" for what students meant by any given category name. (See *figure 10-3* for samples of what "Behavior Contracts" look like.)

Explain to the class that this is known as a "Group Agreement." It is a decision made *by* the group, *for* the group. It does not mean that 100% of the group agree with 100% of the contract. A group agreement means that group members either agree with the decision, or can live with the decision. It is important for students to realize that I have group agreements at my job as well. There may be school rules which I feel give too much power to the suboptimizers. However, I do not feel negative strongly enough to leave the system, so I choose to stay and abide by the rules of the group. It's a compromise I can live with, otherwise I should leave the school and seek a job at another school that more closely matches how I feel the rules should be. This is a new idea for many students. They actually think that as a teacher, I get to make *all* the rules (probably because that is the way many classrooms are run).

Now here is a critical point. Say to the students, "If you feel you cannot live with this group agreement, please let me know and I will do my best to help you drop this class. It is not an option to stay in this class, and refuse to abide by the group agreement developed *by* classroom workers *for* classroom workers." Students are shocked by this offer. I have NEVER had a student ask to leave the class for this reason. The power of the peers is a wonderful thing when it works *for* you!

The culminating activity is to have each student, row by row, or table by table, come up and sign below the "Behavior Contract." Explain that if one chooses not to sign the contract, it does not mean that person is excused from abiding by the contract. However, by signing, classroom workers are showing their support for the contract they have developed. Every person usually signs. Another interesting thing happens on a regular basis. If I have not already identified the potential suboptimizers, I can usually just look at the contract. They almost always sign their name in really big letters. Wanting attention is a hard thing to let go of!

One last thing—I have seen teachers do this activity, then roll it up and store it in a cupboard. This is a HUGE ERROR. If we want students to honor the contract, we must value it by putting it up in the classroom. There have been many times when simply referring to the contract will bring a suboptimizer back in line with a "Sorry Mrs. LaBelle."

Of course, there must be consequences for the die-hards. The first time a student violates the contract, I have them stay after, read the entire contract to me and tell me the part they have broken. It's amazing how much more quiet and respectful a student is one-on-one. I then let the student know that if the contract is violated again, the privilege of sitting by a friend will be suspended for two weeks. (I write the date of moving on the seating chart inside the colored folder. It is the STUDENT'S responsibility to remind me when it is time to move back by the friend. Then I will check the chart, and grant the request if at least two weeks have passed with good behavior.) If the student has honored the contract during the two week time, they may again sit by the friend. If a second move is required, it will be for the remainder of the semester.

One year I had a student staying after school to finish some work for another class. After she finished, we were visiting. She started staring at the "Behavior Contract" and said, "You know, if you would have TOLD us we had to follow all those rules, there's no way it would have worked. But, since WE told YOU it worked really well. I want to be a teacher some day, and if I do, I'm going to use a Behavior Contract!" Moments like that are few and far between, but BOY DO THEY STICK IN OUR MEMORY AND OUR HEARTS!

This is great "stuff." However, if you are like I was, when I first heard of the "Behavior Contract", I was a little unsure of using a new technique AND this new idea of student-generated Behavior Contracts. If you would like to get some practice with the technique before using it to develop behavior expectations, I have a few ideas to get you started. These types of activities will develop skills for you and for your classroom workers.

One year I was teaching high school and I was asked to teach Washington State History. In Washington, all students *must pass* Washington State History in order to graduate. So, the class was not in my area of academic specialty, but it was a management challenge class made up of special education students, English-as-a-second-language students, students who had flunked the class at least once, new students to the state and two students who were in school rather than in jail (the judge gave THEM a choice). What can I say folks? Sometimes when a person is a good classroom manager, the reward is—"you get to teach the really difficult classes to manage!" Even subjects that one hasn't studied since taking that one college class.

We were working on the wagon trains section of the course. I grouped the students randomly and used the *Affinity Diagram* process with the focus question, "Tomorrow I will magically transport you back in time to St. Louis. You will be traveling for the next few months by wagon train to Spokane. What will you take?"

Folks, it was amazing. Students who had never taken part in an activity were actively involved. ESL students were helping others who spoke the language even less. This was the *only* activity participated in by the two students who were in my class rather than be in jail. There was on-task noise and a lot of laughter.

I had each table group of five or six do the post-it note three minute brainstorm activity. Then each table did their own butcher paper with categories. After each table group finished their butcher paper, they presented their *Affinity Diagrams* to the class, and we taped the charts on the wall. We then talked about the similar categories on the different sheets of butcher paper and what kind of restrictions we might consider. For example, a machine gun might give one superiority—until the bullets ran out! Did everyone remember that a wagon was about the size of a conversion van? There was not much room.

On a humorous note, female sanitary products and contraceptive pills were on every list. Some students said if they couldn't take those items, they would hide so I couldn't find them on the "magic" day!

The chart really stimulated lots of thinking. The next day, we reviewed the parameters of size, how long something would be useful and basic requirements for wagon train travel. We then took a look at the previous day's charts—no more input from me. Then I asked them to create a new butcher paper chart using the *Affinity Diagram* technique. Their growth in wagon train packing and *Affinity Diagram* usage was amazing! Also, I became more convinced that this was a good process—ALL THAT STUDENT INVOLVEMENT AND NOT ONE PAPER TO CORRECT!

A few weeks later, in that same class, we used the *Affinity Diagram* as a large group to develop a chart on the quality expectations for a written report on cities in Washington state. Once again, it worked great! The chart was posted so all could see how to earn an "A" paper. I used their posted "A" paper quality expectations to grade the reports. It made my life easier (no arguments on the grading procedure) and the students knew *exactly* what they were being graded on before the paper was turned in. The word "rubric" is now used in education for this idea of clear expectations regarding an assignment's quality standard. In many classrooms the *teacher* spends a lot of time developing the rubric. Please remember: ***STUDENT* DEVELOPED EXPECTATIONS ARE A POWERFUL THING.**

Figure 10-1

Sketch of Radio Choice Post-it Activity

Period 3 Radio Choices

106	88.5	93.7	92	107	105	99
106		93.7	92	107	105	99
106		93.7		107	105	99
		93.7		107	105	99
		93.7		107		99
		93.7		107		99
		93.7		107		#3
		#2		107		
				#1		

Remember, before the vote, Let students know if there are school rules against certain types of music. Be sure you share the reasons for the rules.

Sandy

Figure 10-2

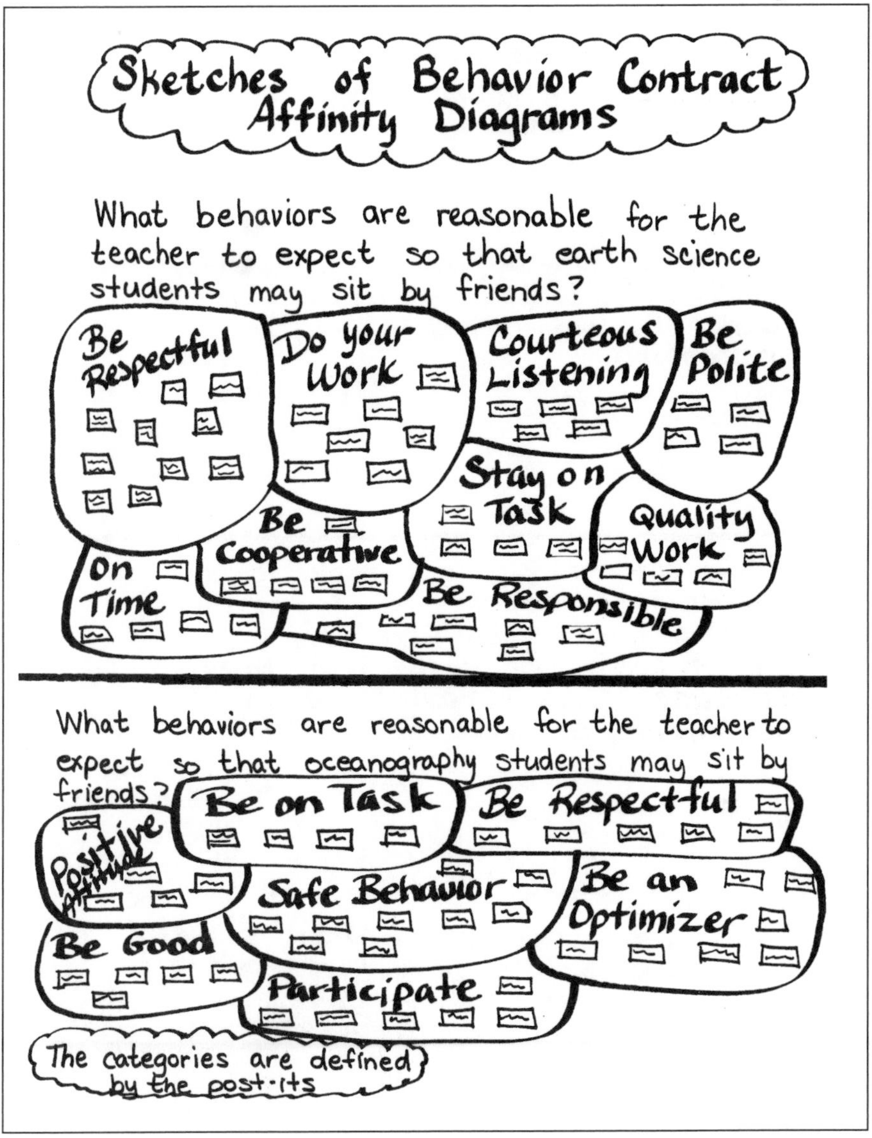

Sketches of Behavior Contract Affinity Diagrams

What behaviors are reasonable for the teacher to expect so that earth science students may sit by friends?

Be Respectful
Do your Work
Courteous Listening
Be Polite
Stay on Task
Be Cooperative
Quality Work
On Time
Be Responsible

What behaviors are reasonable for the teacher to expect so that oceanography students may sit by friends?

Be on Task
Be Respectful
Positive Attitude
Safe Behavior
Be an Optimizer
Be Good
Participate

The categories are defined by the post-its

Figure 10-3

Sample Behavior Contracts

What behaviors are reasonable for the teacher to expect so that earth science students may sit by friends?

Be respectful, Do your work, Courteous listening, Be polite, Stay on task, Quality work, Be cooperative, On time, Be responsible

Student Signatures Here

What behaviors are reasonable for the teacher to expect so that oceanography students may sit by friends?

Be on task, Be respectful, Positive attitude, Safe behavior, Be an optimizer, Be good, Participate

Student Signatures Here

Note: These are words from actual charts ~ The pictures did not turn out well. :(Sandy

CHAPTER 11

How to prioritize classroom group decisions

Sometimes all we need is a collection of group responses, as in the case of the Behavior Contract. Many times, though, we need to prioritize the responses. Do not make the mistake of thinking that a category with the most post-it notes is the most agreed upon or desirable category. The category with the most post-it notes is simply the one easiest to think of. Sometimes I hear people say, "Wow, I never thought of that, that's a good idea!" when they see a new category suggested by another table group.

Once all the categories are up, it is useful to have some type of group method to put them in 1, 2, 3 order. Guess what? I just happen to have an easy, total participatory way to do that task! (Aren't you surprised?) This technique comes from David Langford and Dr. Deming.

The first time I use the prioritizing tool is after we have done an *Affinity Diagram* on the focus question "What activities best help you learn?". Usually this focus question will end up with an *Affinity Diagram* listing about ten to fifteen categories. I do the *Affinity Diagram* on one day and the prioritizing activity the next class day.

The prioritizing activity is called the *Nominal Group Technique* (or NGT). Once we have an *Affinity Diagram,* I share with students that it is very difficult to have a meaningful prioritizing activity for say, eleven topics. "What's the difference between a six and a seven? Not much. So, instead, I want you to pick out *your* top five from the *Affinity Diagram* list of categories." (Before class, I have put the *Affinity Diagram* categories on a sheet of plastic. I number the categories for identification purposes only. Then I show the students the numbered *Affinity Diagram* categories on the overhead.) After students have picked their top five and written them on a sheet of paper, I ask them to prioritize their five picks. "Give five points to the category you most like, four points to the next, and so on until you give one point to the least favorite of *your* top five choices. Give the *most* points to the choice you value the *most*."

To report their choices to me, I have each student take out a *full* sheet of paper. (What is it with kids wanting to turn in a ripped corner of paper for their vote?) I explain that I need a full sheet because I always save the raw data for class decision making, and it is much better if all data is on a full sheet of paper. (Share the purpose.) On the paper, I ask students to make a three way T-chart. The first column has the number of the choice from the *Affinity Diagram* list of categories, the second column has the words of the category they picked, and the third category tells the number of points the person wants to give the choice. Be prepared to show examples the first time or two you do this activity, for all our visual learners. For those of *you* who are visuals, I have included a sample on *figure 11-1* at the end of this chapter. After students have completed their input, have them turn the paper in to the green box by the Teddy Bear.

Once again, BE SURE YOU ALLOW A CLASSROOM WORKER TO TELL YOU THE DATA, WHILE YOU RECORD IT IN FRONT OF THE ENTIRE GROUP. The less the classroom manager touches the data during the creation and analyzing tasks, the more credibility the conclusion has with the workers.

As with the *Affinity Diagram,* classroom workers are usually attentive during the data collection process. One of the classroom workers reads me the category number, the category name and the points awarded. I record this data on the overhead, for example, "Number two, group work, five points." This process continues until all papers have been read. If someone did not follow directions, we do not spend *our* time trying to figure out what *they* meant. They have the choice of redoing the vote or not having their vote counted. (Remember, help—but do not enable.) There is a sample of what an overhead summary might look like on *figure 11-1* and *11-2* at the end of this chapter.

After all data has been recorded, we add up the number of points that each category has received. The next day I will have made a neat chart showing the categories in the order of importance, as voted on by the workers. After the words, I include the vote total number. (There is a sample on *figure 11-3* at the end of this chapter.)

I share with the students, "You have given me input on the ways you best learn. I will try hard to include at least *one* of the top five methods in our daily lessons." Then make sure you do! (This is especially important for the first few weeks. Remember, you are setting a trust foundation here.)

Almost every year, one of the top five student choices for "What activities best help you learn?" is "field trips." The old solution to this vote would be for the *teacher* to decide what field trip to go on. Then the *teacher* would do all the planning, and *give* the students the opportunity to go on the field trip.

In a *Teaching Smarter* classroom the "field trip" vote is an opportunity for students to get a glimpse into the realities of how much work a field trip is. What I say is, "Part of the classroom manager's job is to facilitate the needs of the classroom workers. You have told me, through the NGT, that "field trips" is high on your list of needs. To be honest, if it is up to me, and me alone, you will probably not get a field trip, not because I do not want to, but because it is a lot of work—and I am already *very* busy. However, as your classroom manager, what I WILL do is help YOU get a field trip. We need at least three volunteers to be on a field trip committee. The committee's job is to research at least five field trips (when the site is available, how much the trip will cost, the site's rules for class visits, etc). Then the committee will report back to the class, and we will do an NGT on the suggested field trips. Once the trip priorities have been established, I will access the system for permission slips, possible department money available and bus schedules."

In three years, I have not had ONE student-planned field trip. Yes, they really *want* a field trip, but usually *they* are too busy to meet and plan. However, when one of their classmates expresses unhappiness that no field trip has happened, the blame falls on the committee, not me. The committee members get very defensive about how busy they are, and how the complainer is welcome to be on the field trip committee! Do you see how this plan raises their awareness of the job? Do you think students would be as understanding if the *teacher* were to say they had been too busy to plan the field trip? This is a GREAT learning experience—grab it!

Likewise, if a class ever does get a trip planned, I will be happy to hold up my part. You know what? I'm willing to bet the class would be much more appreciative and well behaved than they would be if the teacher had done all the field trip planning work. Additionally, students have had their awareness raised about how much work planning a field trip is. It is another lesson that THOSE THINGS THAT ARE GIVEN TO US ARE NOT AS VALUED AS THOSE THINGS WE EARN.

I couldn't believe my ears at one of my workshops. A teacher said, "There's no need to ask the students what activities best help them learn. They're just kids, what do they know about educational choices. That's my job, not theirs." Wellll, that may be true in the old system, but asking the classroom workers has worked very well for me in the new method of my *Teaching Smarter* classrooms. Not only that, but for several years now, I have been asking students the focus question, "What classroom activities best help you learn?' and the answers have very closely matched what current research is saying. The responses usually include such things as "group work, working with friends, field trips, discussions, some book work, work in class." These are not hard requests to honor! Keep in mind, I did not *abdicate* leadership with this activity. I *delegated* decision making. I took data from the workers. I committed to try and use at least one of the top five suggestions each class period. It is not hard to do, and it is an incredible tool for student cooperation through involvement!

Another time I use the NGT is when I ask for student input regarding what order I should teach something in. In some classes, I realize there is a certain order in which subjects must be taught. However, many times there is flexibility. Whenever you can offer a choice to your classroom workers, do it. For example, in physics I cannot offer too much choice in the order the subject is taught. However, between Thanksgiving and Christmas, I like to teach astronomy. It applies the concepts previously taught—but it does not *have* to be taught. Although it is an application unit, it does take time from our forward progress in the book. These students are mostly college prep. They sometimes are concerned that they won't "get it all." Therefore, I ask the focus question, "Should we take time from our busy schedule to teach astronomy during the time between Thanksgiving to Christmas?" All I need is one post-it per student. The classroom worker just writes "yes" or "no." "Yes" means "take time for astronomy", "No" means "let's continue progressing through the book and learning new concepts." Couldn't I just have a show of hands? Of course, but I want to reinforce the data collection method, and sometimes there are outspoken people who ridicule those who do not vote as they did. In addition, with a show of hands, the students in front of the class may not see all the voters' hands. There is something powerful about all the sticky notes on the board in columns for all to see.

When I teach earth science, there are more topics than I can ever teach in the time that we have. Also, I do not know what the students have already been taught in lower grades. I choose the topics, then I ask the students to do an NGT. The topics are taught in the order requested. We never get through them all, but we always cover the top four or five. (There is a sample of this on *figure 11-* 3 at the end of this chapter.) What about basic concepts? Those can be woven into whatever topics they choose. Besides, I never get the comment "Why do we have to study this?" because they voted on it! Use your creativity to find ways to get input that is valuable and delegates responsibility, without abdicating leadership.

At about quarter time, I use the *Nominal Group Technique* to ask the question, "Should the difficulty level of this class be increased?' This question was a risk-taker for me the first time. I really had to trust in the classroom workers before I could ask it. I give the students four choices (to make the data easier to analyze).

The four choices are:

- **ABSOLUTELY YES** this class is soooo boring.
- **YES** we could go a little faster. I would like to cover more material in the time that we have.
- **NO**, the pacing is just fine. I am learning but not frustrated.
- **ABSOLUTELY NO**, are you kidding! I'm barely keeping up as it is. In fact, I would like you to go slower.

The students use a post-it and simply write one of the dark printed choices. One of the classroom workers then collects the responses and tells them to me while I record them on the overhead. Remember, the complete answer involves ALL students who are taking this subject taught by you. This means the total data may include two or three classes' input. (There is a sample on *figure 11-4* at the end of this chapter.)

It was not as scary as I thought! In fact, this activity was a real eye opener for some of my students. You know how it is, kids talk among *their* friends, who are usually doing as well or as badly as they are. Then they assume "everyone feels like this." The gifted and the very low achievers are often amazed that there are people in the *same class* who feel completely opposite to them! It is outside of their reality that the class is so easy for them and someone else thinks it is so hard (or vice versa).

I have also been grateful for this data when I receive that rare phone call from a physics student's parent who feels, for example, the class is not challenging enough. I can share with them that 79% of the students like the pace of the class, or would like to see it taught slower. The percentages vary, but you can see how powerful the data can be! I always offer to give the unchallenged student more opportunities to be challenged, but you know what —*they never come in!* Once the parents are assured that I *am* meeting the needs of the *majority* of students, the complaint does not resurface.

Summary

Daydream with me for a moment. You are part of a staff in a school with an authoritative principal. All meetings are pre-set. All agendas are set without your input. The principal feels it is his or her job to already know what you need. Your job is to show-up, listen, and do as you are told. The participation is limited to doing as you are told, when you are told and in the way that you are told. If you are late to a meeting, you are docked 2% of your monthly salary. You are never asked for your opinion, unless it is to respond to what the principal has already decided is the correct answer. Let's see is that a daydream or is that a nightmare?

THAT, folks, is what life is like for many of our classroom workers. They are treated as the assembly-line workers of the past. With the best intentions, we are preparing them for the world of the past. By using *Teaching Smarter* techniques, we begin to set the stage for active decision making by all. The worker has at least *some* control and input over the way business is done in *their workplace.*

I have actually had young people say with awe, "Wow, NOBODY ever asked me anything like this before." It almost brings tears to my eyes. They want so badly to be asked. "Just ask me. I want to help. I want to be PART of this system, not just acted on BY the system." Let the 90%+ help you out.

Just like a staff, students do not want to be asked about every little thing, any more than you or I want the principal to consult us about every decision. However, neither do we want to feel like brainless robots who must have every important decision made for us. THE MOST POWERFUL THING WE CAN DO TO REDUCE BEHAVIOR PROBLEMS AND RAISE THE LEVEL OF THINKING IN THE CLASSROOM IS TO INVOLVE THE STUDENT IN IMPORTANT DECISIONS.

Let's take a look at how station WIIFM works in stereo for these activities. Classroom workers make decisions, reflect, evaluate data, share information, respect other's input, reflect originality, base work on given criteria, are creative, solve problems, are analytical and have persistence. Workers are actively involved. The manager needs to spend *some* time developing good focus questions and working with classroom workers to gather and evaluate data. After class, the ONLY paperwork the manager has to process is the making of the chart. In fact, the classroom manager may choose to delegate that job to a few classroom workers (maybe for extra credit?). That's a *whole* lot more fun than reading and correcting stacks of papers!

Figure 11-1

Here is what a student NGT input paper might look like.

Name
Class Per.
Date

Nominal Group Technique Vote

#	Words	Points
4	Field Trips	5
2	Reading	4
6	Hands-on	3
5	Labs	2
8	Talking	1

Here is what an overhead might look like after student input has been gathered for a class.

What activities best help oceanography students learn?

#1 Group Work 5541544215153342544455
#2 Reading 4225323552554
#3 Worksheets 351354
#4 Field Trips 53355534524351113454 44
#5 Labs 214214422322234333
#6 Hands-on 344134422334232
#7 Book Work 4253423
#8 Talking 11225112421111
#9 Video 15233115422221322115

Figure 11-2

What an overhead might look like after student input has been summarized and ranked.

What activities best help oceanography students learn?

	RAW DATA	TOTAL	RANK
#1 Group Work	554154421515 3342 54455	77	2
#2 Reading	4225323 552554	50	3
#3 Worksheets	351354	21	9
#4 Field Trips	533555345 24351113454 44	79	1
#5 Labs	2142144223 2234333	45	5
#6 Hands-on	344134422 334232	44	6
#7 Book Work	4253423	23	8
#8 Talking	1122511242 1111	25	7
#9 Video	152331154222 2132115	46	4

Remember: always total data with the people who give the input.

Figure 11-3

What the NGT wall chart might look like after all student data has been summarized and ranked.

What activities best help oceanography students learn?

#1	Field Trips	(79 points)
#2	Group Work	(77 points)
#3	Reading	(50 points)
#4	Video	(46 points)
#5	Labs	(45 points)
#6	Hands-on	(44 points)
#7	Talking	(25 points)
#8	Book Work	(23 points)
#9	Worksheets	(21 points)

Another sample NGT wall chart

In what order should we study meteorology?

#1	Storms	(105 points)
#2	Climate	(94 points)
#3	Environment	(86 points)
#4	Air Masses	(65 points)
#5	Layers of the atmosphere	(60 points)
#6	Condensation, Evaporation and Precipitation	(40 points)

as the teacher, I can weave #4,5,6 into topic #1 ☺

Figure 11-4

These are actual results from classroom data gathering.

Should the difficulty level of this physics class be increased?

Absolutely Yes (I'm sooo bored!)	7
Yes (We could go a little faster.)	10
No (I'm learning, but not frustrated.)	25
Absolutely No (Are you nuts?)	10

Should the difficulty level of this oceanography class be increased?

Absolutely Yes (I'm sooo bored!)	2
Yes (We could go a little faster.)	2
No (I'm learning, but not frustrated.)	15
Absolutely No (Are you nuts?)	4

Should the difficulty level of this earth science class be increased?

Absolutely Yes (I'm sooo bored.)	0
Yes (We could go a little faster.)	3
No (I'm learning, but not frustrated.)	14
Absolutely No (Are you nuts?)	3

CHAPTER 12

Change "have to" to "want to"

"There's only one *have to* in the whole world." —Lew Tice, The Pacific Institute

I first encountered the concept of changing "have to" to "want to" in a Lew Tice class. Lew Tice used to be a teacher and football coach, married to a teacher. He became interested in positive motivation and in positive self talk. Over a period of time he did a lot of research, quit teaching and became a very wealthy man teaching the power of goal setting and the power of positive self talk techniques. He also developed sets of video tapes to extend his teachings. One of the sets of tapes was developed for people in their teens. I particularly like the tape titled, "How to manage stress." I want to share with you some of the main ideas from that tape. Lew Tice offers classes and video tapes for purchase. Here is the phone number for contacting Lew Tice's business *The Pacific Institute,* 1-800-426-3660.

Mr. Tice teaches that one of the main ingredients for changing "have to" to "want to" is the power of our subconscious. I share with students his idea that the brain reacts the same, whether it is *someone else* telling us we "have to" or if it is *ourselves* telling us we "have to"—the brain reacts the same. Our brain will "help us out" in one or more of three basic ways.

- **We creatively avoid:** "I've got these other things I have to do first."

- **We do slovenly work:** "I don't care about quality, get it over with. We do *just enough* to make the person pushing us to shut up and go away. What's the minimum I can do so I can claim I tried?"
- **We procrastinate:** "I'll start that paper tomorrow."

Do these three ways our brain "helps us out" sound familiar? Haven't we seen it in the work we get from some of our students? I know I have.

If I was going to play station WIIFM in stereo, I knew I had to figure out how to help students see *why* they would "want to" do the work. I knew as long as students felt they "had to," I would never get the quality work I knew they were capable of. You see, once anyone, teachers included, decides to "want to" there is an "attack mentality" that cuts in and our brain will push us to excellence. Another word for "excellence" is "quality", and quality is a big part of what *Teaching Smarter* is all about—*continuous* quality *improvement.*

I discovered that the more ways I could SHARE WITH STUDENTS the PURPOSE of an activity, and how it would benefit THEM, commitment to quality went up. By weaving together:

- the daily Early Work,
- the opportunities for Quality Bonuses,
- tests that were rewards for daily work,
- the student-generated behavior contract
- and decisions based on student generated data,

I began to see a huge difference in changing "have to" to "want to." The Lew Tice three symptoms of "have to" began to disappear.

Lew Tice tells a story about a long distance runner who was going to college and training for the Olympics. The runner came to Mr. Tice with a problem. It seems that every time the young man heard the last quarter mile gun, his lungs would start burning terribly. However, he knew he "had to" finish the last quarter mile. Do you see how he was talking to himself?

In response to the runner's question of what to do to keep his lungs from burning, Lew told him, "I have the solution—but you might not like it. When you hear the gun for the last quarter mile, SIT ON THE CURB. You see, if you sit on the curb, your lungs will stop hurting."

"That's STUPID!" the young man replied. "If I sit on the curb, I'll lose the race!"

"That's true," said Lew, "but you asked me to help you stop your lungs from burning."

"What do you think I run for?" asked the runner.

"I don't know—*tell me.*"

"I run because my parents in Kenya have sacrificed to send me to America to become an Olympic runner. If I win the gold medal, they will give me a cow. That will make me rich in my country."

Lew replied, "You don't 'have to' run, you 'get to' run. No one's putting a gun to your head. Even if someone did, you would still have a choice. You could run or get shot—it's all a matter of choice. You want to run, you chose to run, you get to run—and if you don't want to, say, 'I don't wanna!' and accept the consequences of your choice."

This whole idea of choice is not familiar to our young adults. They feel they are being "forced", and "made" to do things. If we can begin to help them see that *their* lives are a matter of choice—they want to, they choose to, they get to—lots of rebellious behavior problems go away.

I tell students my classroom is a "free choice" classroom. They do not "have to" do anything. The phrase is "Do whatever you choose to do—but accept the consequences of your choices and behaviors." I share with students that the suboptimizer loves the first part of this rule, but not the second part. We need to be better than that. Sometimes students forget that consequences are not always bad. If one does the homework, studies and seeks help when they need it, they will not fail. I share with students,

"Think of those areas in your life where you feel you have to, and if you really DON'T WANT TO, tell people, 'I don't want to.' But accept the consequences of your choices and behavior."

Students are not used to thinking in a free choice way, so I use some of the examples I learned from Lew Tice:

- You do not have to do your homework—you can *choose* to FLUNK.
  Gee, I don't want to flunk.
  Then if you *want* to pass, do your homework

- You do not have to come to school, you can *choose* to be truant and you may go to jail.
  Gee, I don't want to go to jail.
  If you *want* to stay out of jail, go to school.

- *My parents are always telling me what to do. I have to do it.*
  No you don't, you can *choose* to run away.
  Gee, I don't want to run away.
  If you *want* to stay in your home, cooperate with your parents.

There is only ONE "have to" in the whole world. Sometimes I ask students to tell me what it is. For the first few suggestions, I can usually think of a choice—but they don't like it (like the examples above). The ONLY "have to" in the whole world is to die. We all have to die some time, all the rest is a matter of choice. THIS IS SUCH A POWERFUL CONCEPT TO SHARE WITH STUDENTS!

Sometimes when I give an assignment, a student will ask the familiar, "Do we *have* to?"

I always reply, "You do not *have* to do anything in this class."

The student usually says something like, "Well, I mean, is it worth points?"

Then I say, "Oh, yes, if you *want* the points then you *want* to do the work. However, it *is* your choice."

Seize any opportunity you can to reinforce this idea of free choice. The students are not used to thinking they are living on free choice. It is a wonderful tool for responsibility moving-overmanship.

I have included a copy of an overhead sheet on the next page (*figure 12-1*). I put it on the overhead for students to copy as I present the material. Be sure to uncover only one line at a time as you talk to students. This method keeps them focused on what you are saying. Be sure to include something from this overhead page in your next test. Sometimes students think that if the material is not on the test, then it is not important. Remember their inability to see very far into the future, and let station WIIFM play yet one more time!

So, there are two main ideas from Lew Tice.

Learn how to change "have to" to "want to" because your brain is too smart for you. The brain will use one of the three ways listed above to try and get you out of "have to."

**Everyone is living on free choice,
there is only one "have to" in the whole world.**

Figure 12-1

Lew Tice advice on "Free Choice"

A. Try to change your "Have to" to "Want to"

B. "Do whatever you choose to do, BUT accept the consequences of your choices and decisions"

C. If you feel you "Have to" your subconscious reacts in three ways

1. You slow down (procrastinate)
2. You do sloppy work (just enough to make the person pushing you to be quiet and go away)
3. Creative avoidance (I have these other things I need to do)

CHAPTER 13

Why we need to teach to learning styles

" Find the students' learning styles—and then teach to them"
—Harry Wong, a California *Teacher of the Year*

There are many different learning styles inventories. Your counselor or career guidance person can probably help you find one. Try to get an inventory the students have not already taken. The simpler the better. The PURPOSE is somewhat different than the learning style inventories most students have taken. *This* learning styles test is to raise awareness for the *other* learning styles in the classroom. This will be an *other-awareness* learning experience.

After students have taken their personal inventory, the new twist on the information is to share what other learning styles are in the classroom. This is good for student and teacher alike to see. Not surprisingly, I have found that my physics classrooms tend to be more analytical and quiet learners who like to depend on themselves to learn. My earth science classes (designed for students who have not been successful in science, but need a science credit to graduate) tends to have students who need to talk about the learning, and who depend on friends to help them learn. This is why my physics class will be quiet during a class assignment, and my earth science class will be noisy. Both classes are on task, just very different looking and sounding if one walks in on them.

One time I was working with a group of 120 tenth grade students and four teachers in an integrated "school-within-a-school." In an auditorium as a large group, we took a learning styles inventory. We then grouped the students at two opposite corners of the room by their similar learning styles. (One group was basically gregarious and socially oriented, and one group was more independent and self reflective). The gregarious learning styles groups went to the cafeteria, with two teachers. The more self-reflective learning styles groups stayed in the auditorium with the two other teachers. The physical environments were essentially the same (large rooms with work areas spread throughout the space). Students were then asked to form sub-groups of five or six. The task for each sub-group was to plan four educationally supportable field trips for our "school-within-a-school" (one trip for each quarter). The entire sub-group had to agree on the four suggestions. Once suggestions were agreed upon by all in the sub-group, they were to write their suggestions on a butcher paper chart.

In the auditorium, groups were quietly working together. They situated their groups away from each other for privacy. Using a slightly louder than conversational voice, I could be heard clear across the room. In the cafeteria, groups situated themselves close together. The noise was so loud, I could not be heard if I were to use my "playground voice."

I changed places with one teacher at a time. This allowed each teacher to visit both the cafeteria and the auditorium. The difference was startling!

However, once the entire large group got back together and the butcher paper charts were on the wall, *there was no quality difference* between the "noisy" room product and the "quiet" room product. It was a wonderful experience in seeing learning styles at work.

LEARNING STYLE DIFFERENCES DO NOT MEAN QUALITY DIFFERENCES.

In each teacher's classroom, a summary chart of learning styles for *each class* was posted on the wall. This helped the teachers design lessons for the *students'* learning needs. It is not uncommon for a teacher to expect *students* to adapt to the lesson plan. Will that work? Welllll, we can MAKE it work, but it is SO much more work and effort for the teacher. Even after a lot of work and behavior modification by the teacher on the student, the learning is less likely to "stick" if dominant learning styles are ignored.

This shift in lesson design was hard for me at first. I am naturally a quiet learner, who likes to solve problems myself. A noisy environment is not the best place for me to learn. It took some risk-taking on my part to allow students to talk during a class work time. However, by walking around I found that most of the talking was task oriented—and the talking that wasn't could be easily monitored as I walked around. Harry Wong (a teacher of the year in California) says that misbehavior is inversely related to the distance from the teacher—the *more* the teacher is close to the students, the *less* misbehavior there is!

Be sure students keep a record of what their learning styles are. When we did the inventory for the tenth grade in a large group, each student received a three by five card. On the card, they put their first and last name, their learning style, and the major characteristics of that learning style.

Then, each teacher made a small chart of the learning style profile for members in the individual classes they taught. This was easy because students could tell the teacher their learning style by referring to the 3x5 card. The class chart was posted in the classroom (validate, validate, validate). This chart need not be huge. Mine was only about 20" x 20." Next to the chart I posted an 8½ x 11 piece of paper with the description of all the learning styles. You see, the students only remember the descriptions for *their* learning style.

The summary chart helps the teacher, and it helps the students see the reason why some classrooms are so different in "personality." Not all classrooms are created the same, and it is good for students to be aware of this fact. These summaries also help students see the purpose for the lesson development pattern. So, if I were in a classroom with lots of noise and group work, although it is not my style, I can see that it is the style of most of my classmates. Otherwise, I might think, "My teacher is not a good teacher because the classroom is frequently noisy, and everybody knows it needs to be quiet to learn."

Anytime we can build awareness for students so *they* understand the underlying purpose for our teachings, we are going to have more cooperation and less support for suboptimizing behavior. And THAT my tired friends, is a most wonderful thing!

CHAPTER 14

Substitutes will love coming to your room

Most teachers are rarely absent during the first month of school. Most students, also, are usually in class the first month. This gives us a solid chance to learn and get used to the main concepts of a *Teaching Smarter* classroom. I'm now going to show a way to use *delegation of responsibility.*

After the first month, if I have to be absent and I know about it a day in advance, I can set up a "structured for success" system that works for the students and the substitute alike. Once again, I *change the words* used to *change the concept* about something the students have experienced in their previous school experiences. I change the word "substitute" to "guest teacher" or "guest classroom manager."

I share with students that when we have a guest in our home we treat that person differently than someone who is in our home frequently. For example, we do not expect our guest to know where the towels or the water glasses are. Therefore, when the guest asks where something is, we are patient and explain where to find it, or we get it for them. The same is true for a guest teacher. Why would we expect the guest teacher to know where the worksheets are or how the teacher usually collects the papers? To build on the idea that the guest in our classroom needs our assistance, I put the "guest host or hostess" technique into effect.

The student guest host or hostess is someone who is willing to come into class a few minutes early on the day of my absence. I usually choose two people (just in case one person is absent, and the students prefer working in pairs). The method of choice is random. I ask students to volunteer. Then I write all the volunteers' names on the overhead. I choose one of the non-volunteers in the class and whisper in their ear the "magic number" between one and a hundred. Then the volunteers give me a number between one and a hundred and I write it on the overhead next to their name. After all volunteers have given a number, I ask the non-volunteer student to tell the class the "magic number." (Once again, I distance myself from the power position of knowing the number—thus increasing the credibility that this is a *student* involvement activity.) The two students closest to the magic number are the hosts/hostesses for the day of my absence.

After arriving a few minutes early, it is the host/hostess job to introduce themselves to the guest teacher. (I have also left a note to the guest teacher explaining this process, and the names of the young people who will be the assistants.) After introducing themselves, the host/hostess will go to the folder, get the Early Work and put the papers out on the appropriate table for students to pick up before class begins.

The host/hostess will do the class start count-down, put the plastic schedule on the overhead, turn on the overhead at the appropriate time, take the attendance, and provide any other assistance the guest teacher may need during the period. At the end of the period, the host/hostess will paper clip all appropriate sets of paper together from the day's work, correct the Early Work, put all papers in the file and make sure the correct class dismissal routine is followed. For this job, the host/hostess can earn up to twenty-five extra credit points. It is up to the *guest teacher* to decide how many points the host/hostess will get.

GUEST TEACHERS LOVE THIS APPROACH! After all, as I explain to the students, why should we expect a stranger to our room to know how to run this classroom better than you do—just because they are a grown-up? This is especially the case in a classroom where we are using *Teaching Smarter*. Most adults outside this classroom have never heard of *Teaching Smarter!* It is true that we are required by law to have an adult in the class during my absence, but the classroom workers can run the class in my absence. Here are a few unsolicited comments I have received in the guest teacher report notes:

- "Very good class. All students worked throughout the period." (Remember, these are 103 minute periods!)
- "This class was excellent!"
- "Great group!" "Nice kids!" "Terrific group!" "I've had a delightful day. Call me anytime."
- "Kyle and J.Q. were fantastic! Nice group, they did a super job."
- The students have been cooperative and on task. Great class—as always!"

I don't know about you, but before I began using *Teaching Smarter* techniques and the host/hostess idea, I did not get notes like this from my guest teachers! The notes were nice (after all they want a job!), but never as enthusiastic as the notes I now receive on my return.

THE CLASSROOM WORKERS LOVE THIS APPROACH! Most of them comment that they have never been given this kind of responsibility. They do a great job! I have had times where one of the host/hostess people is absent, and the remaining host/hostess does the whole "magic number" thing to get a partner. They frequently will take over the whole class, leaving the guest teacher as an observer. Let's face it, we all leave practically "goof proof" lessons for our guest teachers anyway. Why not let the students feel the responsibility of leadership? Of course, they are nervous at first. However, after the first few times, there are more than enough volunteers. I even have students asking me if I plan to be absent anytime soon.

Hmmmm, maybe this stuff is working too good!

In the spring of one year I was assisting a teacher in our school with some classroom management techniques. I had the host/hostess pair in my classroom with a guest teacher, and the classroom workers knew I was on campus in case they needed me. Wellll, it was spring and the guest teacher had taken allergy medication. It seems that he sat at the back of the room while the students ran the whole 103 minute period. Not only did he sit at the back of the room—but HE FELL ASLEEP. At the end of two out of our three periods that day, different students came by the room where I was. They wanted to tell me, rather indignantly, that "The guest teacher fell asleep during class!" They were incensed that *he* "wasn't doing it right!"

The fact that he fell asleep was not cool, but the fact that no one outside the classroom knew about it, all the work I had left to be done was completed, paper clipped and in the correct folder with the room neat and clean was REALLY COOL! I did inform my administrator of the sleeping incident, but I spent a whole lot more time bragging about my students! I also shared my bragging with the students. I wanted them to know how proud I was of them for "stepping up" to the situation and acting so maturely. They went from being unhappy about the sleeping guest teacher to being happy with their behavior and the fact that I bragged about them to my boss—and that's a much nicer memory!

One more short story. I had to be absent on a Friday. As in many districts, Friday can be a very hard day to get guest teachers, there is so much demand. Somehow, during the mad shuffle of classroom coverage, no guest teacher was sent to my room during the first period. The error was not discovered until my return on Monday when my students told me with a giggle and with pride, that they had closed the door and conducted the class all by themselves! This is not a situation we want happening on purpose. However, it does show how *much* these young adults love to take the responsibility, if *we* can just structure the expectations and delegate the meaningful task.

There you have it. I guess we can call this *WIIFM in surround sound!* I'm happy because the class is run in a way that makes my return easier. My students are happy because their routine is not disrupted and they are treated as adults with adult responsibility. (Isn't that what we all want?) Two students are *very* happy because they earn up to 25 extra credit points. My guest teacher is happy because it is one of the easiest assignments they could ask for and there are rarely any behavior problems—that makes my boss happy.

One more benefit. I don't know about your district, but in my state we have gone from having a problem finding good substitutes to having a problem finding ANY substitutes. With the method I have just explained, I rarely have a problem getting a guest teacher. Sometimes, they will reschedule in order to take my classroom. It's easy money. I've even had other teachers come to me saying their guest teacher requested that they talk to me about how to do the substitute lesson plans. It seems guest teachers get more assertive when they are in short supply!

In my school, if we run out of substitutes, we begin to pull people off their planning times to cover classes. Let's face it, folks, full time teachers do not make very good guest teachers! I don't blame anyone, for it *is* the "pits" to lose one's planning time, especially when you don't know about it until ten minutes before the bell rings. With the system I have outlined above in place, it is frequently *my* class that will get the different teacher each period. I have actually had my guest teacher pulled from my classroom and assigned to a more difficult classroom, because administrators knew my students could "pull it off."

Allow me a moment to wonder. Why is it the system sees a successful program or teacher at work and, rather than teaching that successful program to all teachers, the system simply USES the successful program or teacher? What are we rewarding, and what are we punishing? We need to be better than that! Systems come in two basic types.

- One system USES up its people. In this system good people and programs are used up, then the system has to rehire when the person burns out and the successful program leaves with them.
- The other system DEVELOPS its people. The best parts of the system are duplicated through training. That way if one person leaves, the system does not lose all the wisdom of that person. Also, training new individuals becomes easier because many people know the successful methods. Therefore, there is more than one source for learning.

At first, I was thinking this "using up people" system was a *Mystery of Life*. However, a *Mystery of Life* is something that seems to have no logical cause. I believe the "uses up people" system is caused by leadership that is so busy managing by crisis, it is unable to plan, lead, organize and direct the FUTURE successes of the system. The focus is on trying to patch the current system to keep it "afloat." Don't get me wrong, I am not putting the blame on our principals. After all, if they did not spend so much time on students "sent to the office" they would probably have more time to plan, lead, organize and direct. Blame may be briefly satisfying, but it is not the route to solution. We can all work together to do better! I like the saying, "It's not WHO is to blame, but WHAT is to blame and how can we ALL WORK TOGETHER to fix it?"

Thank you for your patience during the previous two paragraphs. I guess you can tell I get frustrated at times. These skills are not magic. THEY ARE TEACHABLE. So here I am in my own little way trying to reach as many people as I can with some ideas that I know will work. I'm trying to be "part of the solution and not part of the problem."

Conclusion

Here we are, my new friend, at the end of our visit. I've shared many ideas to increase student responsibility, decrease teacher paper work time, increase the class time spent on higher level thinking skills and reduce teacher stress. I know the changes these ideas made for me in my classroom life. I wish the best in changes for you too.

Here are 26 of the main ideas from Part Two. Check yourself for learning.

- Deviant thinking (educationally speaking)
- Classroom Manager
- Classroom Worker
- Fred Pryor
- Bill Onckin
- Steven Covey
- Jim Rohn
- David Langford
- Dr. Deming
- Total Quality Management
- Quality Learning
- The real product of schools
- Suboptimizers
- Process vs product

- Questions for student data collection
- Higher level thinking skills of this method
- Debrief
- Name Game
- Bears in the Air
- Get the Time Down
- People Puzzles
- How to choose a radio station
- Affinity Diagram
- Behavior Contract
- Suboptimizing consequences
- Nominal Group Technique (NGT)
- Changing "have to" to "want to"
- Teaching learning styles
- Guest Teacher
- Student host/hostess
- WIIFM in surround sound
- Two basic types of systems

In my workshops, participants have shared a desire to see what my first four days of class might look like. Now that you know the basics of *Teaching Smarter,* I want to share those plans with you. Once again, these ideas are shared as a suggestion. You will use your creative expertise to fit these ideas into your subject matter and length of class. Remember, these plans are for a 103 minute class period. However, by using these *types* of plans, you can make the first few days of school much less stressful. No matter how many different preparations you have, the first few days are all essentially the same!

DAY ONE

(1)	0 class minutes	Before class begins, have an overhead plastic on the projector that welcomes students and lets them know what class they are in, who the teacher is, what time class starts and where they can sit.
(2)	10 minutes	Take the attendance out loud.
(3)	15 minutes	Introduce the basics of *Teaching Smarter.* (be sure to include an explanation of the Skeleton Schedule)
(4)	15 minutes	Introduce Early Work, model how to set up the paper, and show where to turn the paper in. (I suggest the "Why are you taking this class" question discussed earlier in the book.) After Early Work is completed, show where papers will be before class next time. Then use the overhead to collect and display the class response
(5)	15 minutes	Do the *Name Game* and introduce (and conduct) the Debrief.
(6)	10 minutes	Discuss directions for the *Pipe Cleaner Introductions.*
(7)	30 minutes	Students do about half the introductions in front of the class.
(8)	5 minutes	Introduce the "End of Class Expectations."
(9)	*3 minutes*	Reminder of tomorrow's Early Work expectations. Remind about the seating chart tomorrow. Do the closure technique.

TOTAL = 103 minutes

DAY TWO

(1)	0 class minutes	The music is on. The overhead reminds students that today is seating chart day. Yesterday's graded Early Work is at the agreed spot for pick-up before class begins.
(2)	5 minutes	After the bell rings, Early Work #2 is on the overhead, as part of the filled in Skeleton Schedule.
(3)	10 minutes	Attendance is taken out loud for the last time.
(4)	30 minutes	Finish the *Pipe Cleaner Introductions.*
(5)	10 minutes	The teacher shares diploma, degrees and certificate for teaching, pictures of the family. Teacher tells a little about the teacher as a *person.*
(6)	15 minutes	Do *Bears in the Air* game and Debrief.
(7)	10 minutes	We all make the seating chart. (Teacher explains about the 25 point extra credit opportunity.)
(8)	5 minutes	Teacher shares the "pretty" Early Work chart of students' responses to the first day's question.
(9)	5 minutes	Do the radio station choice activity.
(10)	10 minutes	Distribute books and make book covers.
(11)	*3 minutes*	Do closure and end-of-class technique.

TOTAL = 103 minutes

DAY THREE

(1)	0 class minutes	The music is on, yesterday's graded Early Work is at the agreed spot for pick-up before class begins.
(2)	5 minutes	Early Work for students while teacher takes attendance from the seating chart.
(3)	25 minutes	Book tour and some reading out loud from the book's introduction chapter, on a volunteer basis. (This is where I explain how each student volunteer will receive an extra credit point, which is recorded on the seating chart. These extra credit points will be added to the seatwork half of their grade at semester.)
(4)	20 minutes	We do the *Get the Time Down* game and Debrief.
(5)	25 minutes	We discuss the Lew Tice "Free Choice" ideas.
(6)	10 minutes	Students write a letter to me about learning needs and anything else they feel comfortable sharing.
(7)	10 minutes	Teacher reviews the Quality Standards for an in-class break—then the class takes a 5 minute in-class break.
(8)	5 minutes	I set the scene for the Affinity Diagram process we will do next class.
(9)	*3 minutes*	We do the closure and end of class technique.

TOTAL = 103 minutes

DAY FOUR

(1)	0 class minutes	The music is on, yesterday's graded Early Work is at the agreed spot for pick-up before class begins.
(2)	5 minutes	Students do Early Work and teacher takes the attendance.
(3)	10 minutes	I introduce and model the Quality Standard Bonus.
(4)	25 minutes	Students do a Quality Standard Bonus written activity while the teacher introduces and uses the *Teacher Prowl.*
(5)	5 minutes	We take an in-class break.
(6)	10 minutes	I describe the Affinity Diagram process for creating the Behavior Contract.
(7)	10 minutes	Students create data and categorize at table groups.
(8)	20 minutes	Students create and record large group butcher paper categories.
(9)	15 minutes	We do the *People Puzzles* game and Debrief.
(10)	*3 minutes*	We do closure and end of class technique.

TOTAL = 103 minutes

There you have it, the first four days in my classroom. See how the schedule is *very heavy* on process and *very light* on subject specific activities? By the fifth day, the process for the class is firmly set, names are memorized by all and we are ready to use class time efficiently. I do not feel that learning time has been "wasted." Rather, we will more than make up for not jumping into content the first day by the efficient use of class time from the fifth day on. Give this a try at least once. I bet you will never have a more relaxed beginning of school, and your students will be happier too. I have found that happy classroom workers are not usually behavior-problem workers!

Epilogue

If you are just beginning your journey as a teacher, you now have a ready-made "bag of tricks" to help you through the first couple of years. I want you to BEGIN close to where I ended in management skills. After all, it is always easier to modify someone else's ideas than to create them in the first place.

If you are an experienced teacher, I hope you have found a few ideas to make your days in the classroom a little easier. Many of us are asked to mentor a new teacher—as we also work full time in our own classrooms. Although some of the ideas in this book may not have been new to you, perhaps I have put them into words that will make the sharing easier. I agree that as experienced teachers, we should "share the wisdom" with our new colleagues. I also know how the best of intentions can get buried as we get busy in our own classrooms, and the new teacher is too shy to "bother us."

It is my hope that this book will begin the pattern of "Continuous Quality Improvement" for at least some of my friends in the teaching profession. One of the hardest pieces of advice comes from David Langford in his *Quality Learning Seminars*. "Work on your own sphere of influence, and, if the change is good, word will spread." Begin with your own classroom and with the new teachers you mentor. It takes time, but word WILL spread.

I'm writing this book after four years of expanding my sphere of influence.

Sometimes I feel like giving up. It is sooo much extra work to set-up and schedule seminars, not to mention the stress of "stand and deliver" in front of one's peers. But I *have to* be better than that, and so do you. How can education truly improve without the wisdom-sharing of its successful experienced teachers?

Too often, the teaching profession is like a conveyor belt. We begin our classroom life at one end and move slowly through the years. We go through the trials and tribulations of experience, and just as we get *really good* at it, we fall off the end of the conveyor belt—we retire. Too often the wisdom falls off the end of the belt along with the retiring teacher. The new teacher begins waaay back at the *beginning* of the conveyor belt of experience.

If we do this whole thing "right", the new teacher begins much closer to where the retiring teacher left off. We MUST share the wisdom. That's "Continuous Quality Improvement," NOT continuous *reinvention.*

With flexibility and "Continuous Quality Improvement" we will be successful. Nobody works harder to do what's best for our children than their parents and their teachers.

Good luck to you. I hope you know I wish you all the best.

Remember—Stereo WIIFM!

TEACHING SMARTER — BOOK II

is now available!

Learn even more ideas to help reduce teacher stress and fatigue, while increasing student responsibility.

Sandy's second book is written in the same conversational tone you have enjoyed in this book, with stories and examples to keep the learning alive and related to the "real world" of working with young people!

TITLE	QUANTITY	PRICE	TOTAL
Teaching Smarter–Book II		$19.95 each	
Washington Resident Sales Tax @ 8.6%			
(Allow 4 weeks for delivery) Shipping @ $4 each book*			
TOTAL			

Make check payable to: **Sandra LaBelle**

Mail check and order form to: *Teaching Smarter*
25430 162 Place SE
Covington, WA 98042

Please Print

Name ____________________

Address ____________________

____

Phone ____________________

Email ____________________

School ____________________

Purchase Order # (if needed) ____________________

*CHECK **www.teachingsmarter.net**

FOR SHIPPING DISCOUNTS ON ORDERS OF 10 BOOKS OR MORE

(Order form for more Book One is on the next page)

*Would you like more copies of **Teaching Smarter–Book One**?*

TITLE	QUANTITY	PRICE	TOTAL
Teaching Smarter–Book One		$19.95 each	
		Washington Resident Sales Tax @ 8.6%	
		(Allow 4 weeks for delivery) Shipping @ $4 each book*	
		TOTAL	

Make check payable to: **Sandra LaBelle**

Mail check and order form to: *Teaching Smarter*
25430 162 Place SE
Covington, WA 98042

Please Print

Name____

Address______________________________________

____

Phone_______________________________________

Email_______________________________________

School______________________________________

Purchase Order # (if needed)______________________

*CHECK **www.teachingsmarter.net**
FOR SHIPPING DISCOUNTS ON ORDERS OF 10 BOOKS OR MORE

Keynotes, Workshops and
Consulting Services available.
For more information contact:

Sandra LaBelle
at:
Teaching Smarter
25430 162 Place SE
Covington, WA 98042
(253) 630-2907
www.teachingsmarter.net
email: info@teachingsmarter.net *or*
sandra_labelle@hotmail.com

Feedback for Continuous Quality Control

I would appreciate any feedback you would care to share with me. I am continuously improving my services and products. In the event of an additional printing of this book, I would value any suggestions for additions, deletions, changes, corrections, errors, or just general comments. Thank you in advance for your time!

You may also contact me by calling (253) 630-2907, or by emailing me at info@teachingsmarter.net *or* sandra_labelle@hotmail.com

Teaching Smarter has been helpful to me because:

____

____

____

____

____

Teaching Smarter could be improved by:

____

____

____

____

____

Mail to: **Teaching Smarter**
25430 162 Place SE
Covington, WA 98042

CLIP-OUT COUPONS

SO YOU CAN HELP YOUR FRIENDS ENJOY THE *TEACHING SMARTER* MOTTO OF "LESS TEACHER STRESS AND FATIGUE WITH MORE RESPONSIBLE STUDENTS."

To receive *Teaching Smarter* (Book One) and/or *Teaching Smarter* II,
please visit www.teachingsmarter.net and go to the "Order" page.

Thank You!

To receive *Teaching Smarter* (Book One) and/or *Teaching Smarter* II,
please visit www.teachingsmarter.net and go to the "Order" page.

Thank You!

To receive *Teaching Smarter* (Book One) and/or *Teaching Smarter* II,
please visit www.teachingsmarter.net and go to the "Order" page.

Thank You!

To receive *Teaching Smarter* (Book One) and/or *Teaching Smarter* II,
please visit www.teachingsmarter.net and go to the "Order" page.

Thank You!